Shrewd Business for the King's Business

SHREWD BUSINESS

FOR THE

KING'S BUSINESS

CROSS-CULTURAL LESSONS FROM THE SOUTH SEAS

CALEB COPPENGER

NASHVILLE

NEW YORK • LONDON • MELBOURNE • VANCOUVER

SHREWD BUSINESS FOR THE KING'S BUSINESS
Cross-Cultural Lessons from the South Seas

Published in New York, New York, by Morgan James Publishing. Morgan James is a trademark of Morgan James, LLC. www.MorganJamesPublishing.com

Unless otherwise noted, Scripture quotes are taken from *The Holy Bible, English Standard Version* (ESV). Copyright 2001 by Crossway, a publishing ministry of Good News Publishers.

Scripture quotations marked NIV are from *The Holy Bible, New International Version*. Biblica, Inc., Copyright 1973, 1978, 1984, 2011.

Proudly distributed by Publishers Group West®

ISBN 9781636984001 paperback
ISBN 9781636984018 ebook
Library of Congress Control Number: 2023951199

Cover Design by:
Rachel Lopez
www.r2cdesign.com

Interior Design by:
Chris Treccani
www.3dogcreative.net

Morgan James is a proud partner of Habitat for Humanity Peninsula and Greater Williamsburg. Partners in building since 2006.

Get involved today! Visit: www.morgan-james-publishing.com/giving-back

To my brothers and sisters in Christ living in Eastern Indonesia

Table of Contents

ACKNOWLEDGMENTS

The content of this book makes it clear that I am indebted to many Indonesian friends who have taught me cultural and spiritual lessons during my time on Buton. They may not have been trying to teach me things, but, as in so many of the challenges that confront us in life, God provides us foundational lessons through everyday situations. I have learned that religion and cultural background are not always the most important indicators of who will become a close friend. I am thinking in particular of two Muslim friends who were crucial in our being able to live on Buton all these years and accomplish much of what is described in this book.

I am also indebted to the church where I worship, and with whom I've lived life all of these years on Buton. There are many pastors and Christian friends in the city whom I count as close friends as well, but the everyday interactions with others out at the farm and in the jungle have reminded me of the strength and dedication required to run a farm and do manual labor. This was especially refreshing during our bi-weekly team building times of clearing land during the COVID-19 pandemic. I don't take for granted the lessons I've learned on these islands, because I don't think there is anywhere else on earth I could have learned them. The island and people of Buton will always have a special place in my heart, the reason that I will always consider it my home away from home.

There are also many Americans, Australians, and Europeans who have impacted me in a significant way during my time in Indonesia, and I have worked with several of them on dilemmas and challenging situations presented in this book. In particular, I would like to thank Michael VrMeer for always being a supporting friend and sounding board while working through issues such as those described in this book. He could probably write a book on his own, and I appreciate the friendship of he and his family for all those years that they lived in the same city with us on Buton. We have had several other Western friends live in the same city as us on Buton during our time there, as well as guests who visited us and the island, who helped keep us sane while living all those years so far from home.

In the writing and editing of this book I am very indebted to several people, especially my dad who has been my primary help in editing it. Even when my siblings and I were young, he would always engage with us over new ideas, and could be trusted to give sound advice and helpful illustrations on a variety of issues. And my mom was always willing to read anything I have written, and be a constant source of encouragement since I was a child. I can't begin to describe how thankful I am to have such parents. I would also like to thank Dr. John Cragin for his timely advice in reordering the book to make it more engaging for businessmen and social entrepreneurs to read. I would also like to thank my Dutch friend, René van den Berg, who always brought me joy on his trips to Buton, and consistently provided sound advice and wisdom. There were several others who read the manuscript and gave advice which only served to make the book better. Any shortcomings in this book are solely my responsibility, and there would have been many more if I didn't have help from all those mentioned above.

Finally, I would like to thank my family, who has lived this adventure with me all these years. I don't know any women besides Tiffany who could do so much to make a home for her family out so far from where she was raised, and by "far," I don't mean just distance. Her passion for others and for acting on what she believes has always been an inspiration to me. And we have been blessed with the greatest children we could ever ask for. I'm amazed at their flexibility, and ability to thrive in any situation where they've been placed. In addition to some of the reasons outlined in this book, another reason many families are not able to stay long term overseas is because of issues with raising and educating children in another culture. My family is truly extraordinary.

I consider the relationships with all of the friends and family mentioned above, as well as with many I have not mentioned, to be a gift from God. I have always held our ability to live in Indonesia loosely, because I know that it could have been taken away at any moment as foreigners living in a foreign land. But the Lord saw fit for us to have quite a run. It is only by His Grace and care for us that these lessons have been learned, and our lives have been so rich while living on Buton.

INTRODUCTION

Needle Rock Venture

In 2011, a venture began in an area called Needle Rock on a remote island in Eastern Indonesia. It started as a community development project, aimed at helping rebuild a remote village destroyed by a wave about thirty-five years earlier. It accomplished these goals, and the area also eventually developed into a primary tourism priority for a city of around 150,000. The business activities associated with this venture worked through two types of locals and in different ways. The first was the long-standing community of Christians (a local church) who had lived in the Needle Rock area intermittently for generations. The second was an informal community of Christian Indonesians (or "near-culture believers") who had moved more recently to the area around Needle Rock from other parts of Indonesia, and were exploring business opportunities on the island. Working together, these two communities of Indonesians, partnering with two expats from the West, were able to establish a tourism foothold in a beautiful, and in many ways untouched, tropical island in

Eastern Indonesia. This is the story of the important principles learned from that successful social enterprise.

After several years of developing relationships with the people of Needle Rock trying to determine how we could work together, we looked toward land acquisition. It's possible for private citizens to own land in Indonesia, and in many of the remote parts of the country proving land ownership means a significant windfall of cash for otherwise poor farmers if they can find an interested buyer. Because of this, there can be significant challenges when it comes to ensuring that one truly has the right to own or use the land. If the land is undocumented, locals must first go through a process of proving that they or their family had previously developed or farmed the land and that there are no valid disputes to this claim within the community. Once their claim is validated by the local district or sub-district, then the process of securing a deed with the local land department can be initiated. If a foreigner wants to buy land, there are several different options. None of these options includes a deed that says the foreigner owns the land, but there are several options where the right to use the land for a significant amount of time can be secured.[1]

In rural parts of eastern Indonesia, the process of obtaining and using land for tourism development is not a purely legal process, but usually requires significant interaction with the local community and a trusting relationship with at least one local individual. In most cases, if the local community does not want a foreigner to develop a certain area, then they will be able to impede that process to the point where it will probably not be worth the effort. This has happened for different reasons in Indonesia, some of which deal with environmental issues involving corporations.[2] But if the development is mutually beneficial in some way for the developer and those in the local community, then it can be a successful endeavor. This provides some accountability regarding the social aspect of the triple bottom line of sustainability ("people, planet, and prosperity"), because without some level of social support the development can have significant challenges both short and long-term. Even when the legal support for land use is in place, there are other social factors that may require ongoing maintenance to reassure nearby local communities that any development will be a net positive contribution to the area in which they live.[3] This case offers background information about Indonesia, specifically a rural community on the island of Buton in eastern Indonesia. It addresses the problems involved with securing land ownership and the right of use; the path to sustainable tourism, and possible broad implications.

Beginning with the details surrounding the business venture in Needle Rock, this book is an attempt to show some ways that we as Westerners may be able to help our employees and surrounding communities, through humility and the assumption of financial risk on our part. These are real situations and case studies from life overseas that helped shape the Seven Levels discipleship tools outlined in the final chapters of the book. This is not meant to be some type of specific pattern for others to follow, but I hope that the ways of thinking illustrated in these chapters will inspire creativity in others about how best to work together with Indonesians, to set them and their families up for success, as many businesses and organizations in the West have helped us. At this point in history, we can address the lack of financial, educational, and social support for Indonesian believers who want to move to Muslim majority areas to be a light for Christ, while raising their families and building a life there. In the Bible there are many examples from the life of Paul during times of cross-cultural life and work, about how he allowed himself to be at the mercy of others, sacrificed some of his personal privacy and sense of security, and tried to set up others for success more than himself. There was often a good level of interdependence between those who came from the outside, and those who were living there.

Usually, those of us from the US who live overseas don't stay there long-term, but try to lead and serve in the short-term, to have maximum positive impact while we are there. This concept has been communicated for many years, as with the acronym MAWL (Model, Assist, Watch, Leave), which also lines up with the goals of the Indonesian Labor Department in that foreigners who work for a business and apply for a work permit in Indonesia are expected to be training up a local Indonesian to take their place. In Muslim majority areas where new believing businessmen and women do not have the means to sustain themselves independently apart from their Christian home community, things such as their identity, assets (such as a house), and a stable income, are very important elements to consider when implementing MAWL. The efforts to reach independent sustainability will probably take a long time, but in most cases we need to focus on small steps forward in that direction. I would argue that the measure of our success as foreigners overseas is not best determined by how long we have lived in a certain area, or how well we master one of the local languages, but more about how we were able to serve and work effectively together with the local church, our employees, and individual believers to help prepare them for accomplishing long-term goals. Language and longevity are important means to accomplishing these goals but are not the primary goals by themselves. "Serving" is not just living in a place that is hard for us; it needs to be combined with an ever-increasing clarity of thought and ability to see how we can best serve our brothers and sisters overseas in such a way that they can truly know they are being served, regardless of cultural background. Jeremiah writes, "But seek the welfare of the city where I have sent you into exile, and pray to the Lord on its behalf, for in its welfare you will find your welfare" (29:7).

Serving others in a cross-cultural context may not always require living in that setting for decades, but there is something to be said for planting your life somewhere outside of your home country in order to have a long-term impact, sometimes for generations. Those in the Muslim world have been doing this for a long time, as we can see in the changing demographics of Europe. The primary motivation is probably economic, in that they have more opportunities and a better quality of life in Europe than in the Middle East. But the results of these moves are not just economic, as Muslims often attempt to further the Islamic agenda where they move. This same thing is happening with large scale movements of Muslim Javanese to places like Papua in Indonesia, where there are many economic opportunities. But, at the same time they are trying to influence Papua for Islam. While Christians know that true religion is more a matter of the heart, I think we know that there are tangible ways we can see what people believe in their heart. I heard a professor at Gordon-Conwell Theological Seminary once say that, while there are many ways we can support overseas ministry financially without ever going overseas, we must not stop sending our sons and daughters overseas. There is something that communicates a higher level of seriousness concerning the commands of Christ and his calling on our lives when we or our family moves overseas. It is also more effective in influencing long-term change if we are willing to do so. Muslims have been doing this for centuries, and while we might question their motivation, we must admit that it is making a large impact. If Muslims will move for economic reasons, and have large scale religious impact, should Christians not make the same sacrifice for spiritual reasons?

Being Shrewd and Possible Pitfalls

While a major argument of this book is that we should be generous with our financial resources, I know there are many potential financial pitfalls which can be extremely harmful to both the Westerners and the Indonesians involved. At the same time, we need to do a better job of not being overly preoccupied with possible financial pitfalls, so much that it paralyzes us. This is where the Seven Levels principles at the end of this book should help us step back from some of our possible hang-ups with money, whether a matter of our being overly protective with our own personal money or being unreasonably fearful of getting in trouble for handling money wrongly. We also need to be wary of not using a "talent" with which we've been entrusted. As in the parable of the "Shrewd Manager" in Luke 16, Jesus says that the people of the world often use their resources in a cleverer way than believers (v. 8). In this connection, I think of a conversation I had with a well-known Swiss German businessman in our province. I asked if he ever worked together with a large NGO (also in our province) that focuses on conservation training, and he said "Once, but never again." It was because they were so used to spending other people's money, they didn't look critically at projects they were involved in to see if they would be profitable and have long-term success. If something sounded good, or seemed like it would help others in some way that would be popular with supporters, they would throw large amounts of money at it and not worry about the results. This businessman did not have that luxury. He said his business would go under if he did not critically evaluate everything he did financially. His livelihood depended on it. He thought that if individuals running that NGO had tried using $10,000 of their own money, they would have acted very differently.

While believers are concerned with eternal goals, as well as earthly ones, it would do many of us good to think more critically about how we use funds with which we have been entrusted with by others. In this parable, Jesus refers to money as "unrighteous." Leon Morris writes, "The use of the term unrighteous money may imply that there is commonly some element of unrighteousness in the way men acquire possessions." And as "well-intentioned as they are, the sons of light (servants of God) often lack the wisdom to use what they have as wisely as the worldly use their possessions for their very different ends."[4] While it may be that in the business world, we see many who have succumbed to the god of "Mammon," we should do our best to serve the Lord using all of our talents and shrewdness, even when business may not seem as spiritual as other activities.

In the parable of the unrighteous manager, many commentators believe that the amounts that the loans were reduced represented interest charges on the actual principle of the loans, and usury was forbidden by Jewish law. So, after this manager was discovered as being dishonest by his owner, he then went and cancelled the mark-ups on the loans that he had charged, which would have probably been his personal profit on the loan, even if part of the interest went to the owner. He did this so that after he was fired, those who had their debts reduced would welcome him into their homes when he was in need. The manager acted honestly, shrewdly, and decisively by reducing the debt to the proper amount before he lost his job, but it was done with selfish intent, and was only done after he was certain he would never get that money. Even though God knows our hearts, in the parable, the owner could not reprimand him for this, or he would incriminate himself as well for charging interest on the loans. The owner (who represents God) commended the unrighteous servant for his shrewdness. "He did not say he was pleased with the unrighteousness of the manager, just that he admired the astuteness of the manager."[5]

To summarize the parable in another way, the manager decided that those who were in debt should just pay what they owed the owner (God), not him. The gratefulness this would elicit in those who now had lighter debts, could pay non-monetary dividends for years to come. Believers are encouraged to act decisively in this way for eternal ends. An Indonesian friend of mine who sells bread has decided to set aside up to five pieces of bread a day specifically for the purpose of giving to people for free while trying to start up a conversation with them. He's making monetary sacrifices for non-monetary gain. The early church did this as well. Referring to the parable of the unrighteous manager, John Sailhamer writes that Luke no doubt took words to mean, "Use worldly wealth to gain friends for yourselves, so that when it is gone, you will be welcomed into eternal dwellings" (v. 9), to speak to the situation in the early church that is reflected in Acts, where the early believers shared their worldly goods with one another (see Acts 2:44-47; 4:32-37).[6] God knows our hearts, and he wants us to be focused on pleasing Him, but not just in a theoretical way. He wants us to be decisive and shrewd in how we use our money, not burying our talents in the sand, but investing in others for eternal purposes.

A very real threat in the world today is reflected in the "prosperity gospel," where material wealth is seen as a sign, and maybe even the goal, of a close relationship with God. This is not a new concept among religions. A very important concept within the spread of Islam in Indonesia was *Martabat Tujuh* (Seven Levels),[7] with the higher levels of holiness pursued in these teachings get temporal and eternal blessing (*berkat*), enabling the holy to get what they wanted by imagining it (or "praying"). Sound familiar? These same things are pursued by many Christians today.

The gospel message is most concerned with how people are forgiven and made right with God, but many Christians are unable to communicate what this right standing with God is for. Many Christian denominations today fill in this gap with saying the closer you are to God the more blessings you will receive (*berkat*) and that your prayers have great power to get you what you want. A large portion of the influence we Westerners wield in Indonesia is because of the economic prosperity of America and our personal prosperity contrasting with that of most Indonesians. Churches in Indonesia are also filled with many rich ethnic Chinese Indonesians, and economically prosperous *pribumi* (ethnically indigenous to the islands of Indonesia). These are all silent and powerful witnesses to one of the popularly understood goals of right standing with God through Christ—blessings, powerful prayer lives, and getting what we want. Being blessed and having more money than we actually need does not disqualify us from teaching the true biblical goals of our faith, but if we are not clear in teaching these biblical goals, there are plenty of "prosperity focused" Christian teachings in circulation to make believers think that Christianity and Islam are alike in their goals—to convince God to give us what we want.

When we add the difficulty of communicating these truths cross-culturally, with all the baggage and accusations of colonialism and paternalism, it can often be difficult for Westerners to know just what they should be doing if they decide to live overseas as Christians in places where there are few other believers. These Seven Levels can guide us as we work together with nationals with humility and understanding and attempt to cut through all the differences in our lives to see how we can each help one another. The following chapters are not only an attempt to build cultural understanding and put forward some possible ways to support Indonesian employees and friends holistically in business ventures, but also to explain how some Indonesian Christians might see us as Westerners. There will always be recurring problems between believers, both within Western churches, within Indonesian churches, and also between Westerners and Indonesians, which are often the result of misunderstanding or an unwillingness to accept risk and lean on the side of humility. I know the issues discussed in the following chapters are very complicated, but I think it is better to offer some material for discussion instead of remaining silent.

I hope that this book can show ways that life lived in light of an understanding of Seven Levels can help us work together in a way that better reflects the unity of the global community of believers.

The Lord is at work throughout the world. We just need to have eyes to see what He is doing, and have a bias for action. Many businessmen and women throughout the world want to use their resources and gifts to help believers in other parts of the world. This is not the work of professional ministers, but of lay people in the church trying to follow the Lord's will for their lives. There might be times where these lay people in the church "don't see results" in their efforts to help other believers; but measuring the achievement of spiritual goals can be a very complex affair. We might not be "seeing results" because we aren't seeing what God is actually accomplishing through us. The results we are having might be right in line with God's goals and our calling, but we may have created a different ideal, one that really isn't from God at all for this time and place. So we can't see clearly and don't value appropriately what He is accomplishing through us. Please read the following chapters with an open mind, and think about how God may be calling you to take steps of obedience which require sacrifice, dealing with unknowns, and making yourself vulnerable in order to be right where He wants you to be.

CHAPTER 1

From Jungle to Villa
In Eastern Indonesia

The Nation of Indonesia

The Republic of Indonesia is a democracy that allows its citizens to own land, but because the nation is spread out among so many islands, there are still large swaths of real estate that are unclaimed.[8] In many cases, individuals own and work portions of this unclaimed land, but they have not gone through the verification process required to obtain a deed to show legal proof of ownership. Since over half of the country lives on the island of Java, historically most of the infrastructure improvement and development on this island is completed using resources generated and provided by the less-populated outer islands. As the outer islands continue to increase in population through the government's transmigration program,[9] with people moving there for new business opportunities, and also through natural population growth, there is an increasing requirement for individuals to obtain deeds. If an individual just plans to live on the land and farm it, then he probably does not need a deed. But if he plans to sell the land or prevent the government from using his for a government project, then they will need to go through the legal process. This is becoming more and more important as Indonesia develops these outlying islands along with increased ease of travel and communication throughout the country.[10]

The Islands of Buton

Buton is an island off the southeastern leg of the larger island of Sulawesi, which used to be the seat of a Sultanate that governed Buton, Muna, Wakatobi, Kabaena, and other surrounding islands. For the purposes of this study, the term "Butonese" will be used to refer to people from any of the islands that used to be a part of the Sultanate of Buton. These islands were an important stopping point for the journey to and from the Spice Islands, which are found among the Malukus in eastern Indonesia.[11] But even though many travelers passed by these islands, not many people stopped to live there unless they were hiding from someone or had been exiled from another kingdom.[12] This changed in 1999 with the violence in the Malukus, as people of Butonese heritage who had lived in the Malukus for generations returned to the land of their ancestors to escape the violence.[13] Even though these migrants usually had at least one Butonese ancestor, they did not have land that was suitable for home construction. So they were looking for land to purchase on the island of Buton, especially near the larger cities of Baubau and Pasarwajo. Many had simply gone abroad to find work and their eventual return led to steadily increasing land prices on Buton beginning around the year 2000.[14] Now with the tourism potential of Baubau and the nearby islands of Wakatobi in play, it seems that land documentation and proof-of-ownership requirements will only increase in the coming years.

Land Ownership in Indonesia

Land that has not yet been legally claimed and documented in Indonesia is considered federal land, but this status is always open to change if an individual goes through the proper process to prove that it belongs to them or someone related to them.[15] As large-scale acquisitions (generally on Sumatra and in Kalimantan) are often associated with palm oil plantations rather than tourism development, this study focuses on small-scale acquisition.[16] Large-scale acquisitions are also subject to environmental deforestation regulations and can be very political.[17] This includes "central government initiatives that result in sudden, large-scale land-use change" by non-local interest groups, activities which can have negative long-term results for the local communities.[18] Even though there are longstanding efforts to increase land certification, only about a third of Indonesia's land is legally owned. The rest is formally owned by the Indonesian state, which often continues the colonial tradition of handing out much of it in the form of concessions to companies.[19] A recent NGO study found that as much as eighty-two percent of the land in Indonesia is controlled by corporations.[20]

The three most important elements in small-scale land acquisition are (1) eyewitnesses who were alive when the land was first claimed, occupied, or farmed by an individual; (2) long term trees planted at the time, ones that still exist and show the boundaries of the land; and (3) a government official at the local sub-district office who can serve as a witness to these physical and verbal verifications of ownership. These officials must ensure the story and details of the land are recorded in an official document that is then forwarded up to the district office for signature. This will provide the foundation for the issuance of a deed at the land office of the metropolitan or regency level of government.[21]

In many cases, the eyewitnesses will be older men and women considered to be the unofficial elders in a community. They will probably have known the person who first arrived on the land and developed it; they can provide details about where that person lived, the types of crops he farmed, and whether there were times that he moved away and why he left.[22] The trees that last for a long time and show the boundaries are typically coconut, and possibly mango, cashew, *kapok, rambutan, duku,* teak, or mahogany.[23] Among the islands of Buton, coconut trees are the best in this connection because the seed is too heavy for a bird to carry. So, if a coconut tree has been planted away from other trees, it was almost certainly planted there by a human. And it was popular because it grows well, and coconuts can be used in a variety of ways for food and drink, for charcoal for fires, and for copra (a source of oil) that can be sold.

Furthermore, shorter term crops like papaya trees, banana trees, corn, pumpkins, and cassava can show that the land was farmed by someone, but their presence is usually not enough to prove actual ownership. Someone could plant these short-term crops while the actual owner was away for a few months or a few years and then try to claim the land as his own.[24] There are also instances where the true owner of the land, the one who planted the long-term trees, gave permission to another person to farm short-term crops there. This is different than traditional profit-sharing arrangement, where the owner is usually richer than the farmer.[25] In these cases, the owner and farmer are relatively equal economically, and if there is no document conceding this right to use, then the person farming the short-term crops may try to claim this land for his own because, while he was farming, no one protested his right to farm it. Such are the conflicts that require local government adjudication.[26]

The Government Role in Land Documentation

The local government officials at the sub-district level wield a great deal of power in sorting out these land ownership stories and details. Their actual role is just to verify that the local elders and interested parties have worked through all the details and come to a conclusion on what seems right to those in the community, but it is often the case that officials try to use their important role for personal advantage.[27] These local government offices take care of many administrative details for the citizens under their jurisdiction, but there are many officials who are also looking for other ways to make money on the side. It is usually culturally accepted for citizens to tip government officials for completed paperwork they require. In some cases, if a tip is not received, the office will still complete the paperwork grudgingly, especially if it is related to the issuance of an identification card, a building permit, or land registration in a person's name for property tax purposes. They're required of everyone, so officials are usually helpful. But if the paperwork will lead to the possibility that an individual will make money in the future, whether through a business license or land-ownership documentation, then it will most likely require some type of informal fee or tip. Still, it must be said that there are instances where the citizens are not charged a fee, which may be an indicator of Indonesia's success in pro-poor growth initiatives.[28]

Those who are documenting land that they've inherited don't usually have much extra cash available, so they may be pressured to give some of this land to the government official to get their paperwork completed. Sometimes, the government official will not complete the paperwork until payment is made, and, in extreme circumstances, he may arrange for the land to be sold to someone else because they know the true owner will never have enough money to document their land. Despite these potential setbacks, when the documentation letter is completed, it needs to be taken up the line to land officials at the city or regency level. Recently, the government introduced the PRONA program to streamline the process by requiring signoff at only the sub-district office; it's typically free, but it can take longer.[29] Still, in some parts of Indonesia, this push to title land quickly ends up putting poor farmers at a disadvantage.[30]

If application is successful, the Land Department will eventually issue the actual deed to the owner and record the plot in their system after it has been measured and staked. This process can also be a lengthy one and will require some money to be paid officially to get the deed. And then there is typically a tip for the officials who take the trip out to survey, measure, and stake the land. All this being said, many people in Indonesia are comfortable with buying land with only a signed and stamped letter validating ownership from the sub-district office, with all the witnesses' signatures, along with a signed receipt on a 10,000 IDR *meterai* (seal), one which contains the details of what was sold and for how much. The buyer will then usually pay for the deed of sale, the process of obtaining the initial deed for the land from the Land Department, and all the taxes associated with the purchase.

Foreign Citizen Ownership of Land in Indonesia

To own land in Indonesia, an individual must be a citizen. But there are several ways that foreign citizens can hold a strong legal claim to the use of land or to own it through documentation of a personal agreement with the owner or through a business arrangement. A relatively new (and the best) way a foreigner can gain use is to take advantage of a twenty-five-year deed available from the Land Department, and it's possible that it may be renewed for twenty or thirty years.[31]

In Indonesia there are basically two categories of businesses—those that are started with foreign capital and those begun with domestic capital. For many years the majority shareholder was required to be Indonesian in both categories, but after changes in 2023, businesses started with foreign capital can have non-Indonesians as majority shareholders.[32] In businesses started with domestic capital, all of the shareholders must be Indonesian citizens. If a piece of property is in the name of a business started with foreign capital, then a foreigner could have a stake in the ownership of this property because he has a stake in the ownership of the business. In some cases, one of the foreign shareholders might have provided all of the capital to start the business and they would have a letter with a local notary documenting the verbal agreement between the Indonesian shareholder and the foreign shareholder that states the foreign shareholder actually owns all the shares of the company.

The profession of *notaris* in Indonesia is like a combination between a notary public and a lawyer who documents property and business transactions. Whenever someone wants to start a business, they go to a *notaris* for the articles of incorporation and federal registration. Some people also rely on a *notaris* to process all their business licenses with local government offices. When someone wants to buy property or execute other important documents, they usually go to a *notaris* for these as well, and a *notaris* can generate letters to "borrow someone's name" or power of attorney to show who has the authority to make decisions. A *notaris* would be the one to execute a document stating that a foreigner is the true owner of all the shares in a company, even if an Indonesian is written as the primary shareholder in the instrument. It's also the way that a foreigner could show ownership of land in the name of an Indonesian individual citizen.[33]

Throughout, it's important to use a *notaris* familiar with both individuals and the area in which the property is located, and, even better, one who was involved in previous transactions regarding the property or business. Since the foreigner is not named the sole owner in any of the official government documents, he could lose his investment in a worst-case scenario. But a document from a respected local *notaris* would be a powerful testament to the actual situation and would probably prevent an Indonesian who officially owned the property from ever selling it because of its legal contention.

Sustainable tourism development and pro-poor tourism around Buton

Sustainable tourism can be defined as tourism that focuses on the "triple bottom line" of the economic, ecological, and socio-cultural aspects of the business. Using this approach, an organization can determine how it is doing at balancing these three elements of sustainability.[34] On this model, the World Tourism Organization (WTO) presses for development that "meets the needs of the present tourists and host regions while protecting and enhancing opportunities for the future. It is envisaged as leading to management of all resources in such a way that economic, social, and aesthetic needs can be fulfilled while maintaining cultural integrity, essential ecology processes, biological diversity, and life support systems."[35]

As a general rule when someone is looking to buy land for a resort or tourism operation, they are going to pay a high price, and many farmers who own large plots on the coast are hoping that a large company or rich individual will pay an exorbitant price, so the seller can live the rest of his life in comfort. Since remote areas don't have real estate agents or any published and regulated real estate prices, sellers will usually just present a price they want. Sometimes these prices are unrealistically high in a sellers' market, so it's best to know the people who live near the land and have enough time to be patient to wait until the owner needs some money, as in a buyers' market. Furthermore, if the seller is a friend and in a tough financial situation, one's relationship with him and the community can be helpful to all parties concerned, consonant with pro-poor values. [36]

Kakwani, Khandker, & Son propose a two-tiered definition of pro-poor growth, [37] one in which only economic growth which benefits the poor proportionally more than the non-poor can be considered pro-poor. Strong pro-poor growth can be relative (where growth reduces poverty and relative inequality) or absolute (when the absolute benefits of growth received by the poor are equal to, or greater than, the absolute benefits received by the non-poor).

Though the development of tourist opportunities and attractions can profit the poor, it is best to not assign pro-poor tourism its own theory and methodology since it is so intertwined with community-based tourism and other pro-poor developments.[38] For instance, agricultural land purchases are a key part of pro-poor growth in many parts of the world.[39] In this vein, the buyer will also become more integrated into that community and, thus, have a higher possibility of developing a socio-culturally-sustainable tourism destination that the local community will want to be involved in and support if difficulties arise.[40] Of course, sometimes relational challenges can arise because of the amount of money involved in land purchases, especially with the poor.[41]

In remote parts of eastern Indonesia there are many beautiful places that have yet to be explored, sites with potential to be first-class tourism destinations. And since many are small islands, the question of sustainability arises.[42] One example of this is Wakatobi Dive Resort on the island of Onemobaa (next to Tomia, wakatobi.com/dive) in Southeast Sulawesi. The owner came out to these islands in the 1990s, found the location he wanted, and established an exclusive, very successful resort. A few years later, Wallacea Trust, a non-governmental organization (NGO) found a spot on the island of Hoga (next to Kaledupa, opwall.com), where they now have been operating a training center for many years, teaching conservation techniques to college students and other researchers during the summer months.

Both endeavors have been successful, but not as investments that could be discovered, developed, and then left to someone else. It's taken extensive cooperation and coordination with the nearby communities as well as some type of ongoing financial partnership. Individuals who have had a financial and/or social stake in the endeavor from the beginning must continue to stay involved in a very intimate way. If these two operations were left wholly in the hands of local managers, they would probably quickly disintegrate because of their reliance on foreign guests from America and Europe. Furthermore, the financial agreements and unique relationships with the local community may not be culturally feasible for a local manager to maintain. Indeed, it's important for the business to be fully integrated into the local community as local initiatives are important to pro-poor tourism efforts.[43]

The city of Baubau has seen one local, sustainable tourism development initiative. It was started and is operated by a small organization of local young people in a Sorawolio sub-district village as it's relied on a government-owned pine forest to offer its activities. They have a small, ropes course that includes riding a bicycle on cables up in the trees and also a zip line. They also offer archery and paintball practice and a small paintball field for competition. There are many selfie-photo sites in the forest, and it seems to be a popular place for people to come when they have free time. It's located beside a campground and climbing tower that was used for a large *pramuka* (like Boy Scouts and Girl Scouts) jamboree many years ago. This is a good example of government support of a local initiative, with rural infrastructure development in remote areas—a pro-poor initiative.[44] On the relatively-nearby island of Bangka, one also finds tourism efforts to both reduce poverty and improve the economic prospects around targeted beaches.[45]

The Dilemma

An American named Chase had lived on the island of Buton in Southeast Sulawesi, Indonesia for many years and was looking for a place to develop a possible ropes course and zip line as well as offer a place where guests could camp out and sleep in a remote location (villa). It would provide nearby opportunities for such water sports as stand-up paddle boarding (SUP), scuba diving, and kayaking. He now operates an adventure tourism company which makes use of this recently developed site. Before this, international guests stayed in the city of Baubau before heading out to more remote areas where they stayed in the houses of residents. There was no need to provide a place for guests to have some organized activities in the jungle, because guests usually just explored waterfalls and mountains around remote villages. But as the business was trying to market more to domestic tourists, it sought to provide a jungle experience and ecotourism activities closer to home, obviating the need to visit the villages and to stay in the homes of residents on other islands. A jungle location that the tourism company could manage internally offered more activity control for shorter tours not requiring extensive coordination with remote communities. It made for a nice option.

Chase decided that he was going to focus on land options in an area where he already had many connections, territory not yet very developed, but with sufficient road networks and friends nearby to keep an eye on supplies. He watched for land to be sold in the area, but none filled the bill. Each of them offered an opportunity to help someone, but each had long-term risks in that success depended on good, ongoing relationships with those outside the circle of familiarity and trust.

The first piece of land was owned by a woman who had inherited a large amount of land and had planted teak trees throughout most of it to show it was hers, even though the trees were clearly less than ten years old. No one contested her right to own the land, because those who had first developed the land many years ago had departed. A few individuals in the area even knew she was not really the original owner, but it was not worth the effort for them to contest it because she had been working it for several years. She was living there, and the former farmers didn't care since they lived in another province. She never had enough money to pay the local sub-district office for the paperwork to prove she owned the land, so it was hard for her to profit from it.

Then one day, she was surprised to learn her son needed to relatively quickly marry a woman because of cultural pressures. In Indonesia the parents of the groom take care of the wedding expenses, and there is usually a bride price to pay, so she needed a significant amount of money in a short period of time. Chase was aware of the situation, and was also friends with the son, so he wanted to help. He knew how much money she needed, and she showed him the land she had available to sell for that amount of money. The piece of land she showed him was very large for the price and in a good location. Even though this was a remote area, Chase felt like he would be taking advantage of her if he bought all this land for that price. So, he worked out in his mind what he thought a fair price per meter would be, and then told her he just wanted about a third of the land she'd offered him, but at the price she'd asked. It turned out that, a few years later, the woman was basically forced to give the leftover two-thirds of land to a local government official in order for the paperwork to be done proving ownership of her other pieces of land. Chase had not wanted to take advantage of the woman's situation, but she ended up being taken advantage of by someone else. He wondered if he'd made the right decision, but he did feel that the other residents in the area thought his heart was in the right place. But his friends would probably have preferred that Chase had bought the whole, large piece of land in the first place. That way, they wouldn't have had a corrupt official as their neighbor (on the other two thirds of the plot), one who'd probably sell the land to someone else they did not approve of.

The second piece of land Chase considered was being sold by a guy that had frequent financial troubles and was not making wise decisions. It seemed like he had turned over a new leaf and needed some capital to start a new chicken farm. He had inherited some land that was clearly his from his father, and he used it to farm for several years. It was a decently sized plot, and Chase was not sure that he needed it all. So, he consulted with some friends in the area to make sure that everything was clear regarding the man's ownership and that he was in a good place to deal with a financial windfall. Things looked good, but Chase decided to just buy half of the land because that was all he needed at the time, and he wanted to see how the man handled the money. The man did end up using the money to invest in a chicken house and buy some chickens, and, several months later, he let Chase know through their mutual friend that he was interested in selling the other half of his land. Chase was in a place financially to buy the rest, and it seemed like the man was still in a good place financially to handle it, so the transaction took place. All along the way, Chase had negotiated the sale with a trusted mutual friend just to make sure there was good accountability. And that way, he could hear of any disputes or gossip about the potential transaction before committing to anything. He knew it was always wise to involve several trusted individuals with a good knowledge of the status and history of land in remote areas, because many of the potential problems are not documented. There may have been verbal agreements and conversations about real estate that could only be verified through close relationships with elders in the local community. Everything checked out, but the seller did eventually lose all the money through a bad bet, and he found himself in a difficult situation. Chase felt bad that this was the final result of the sale and wondered if there was something he could have done better to help him manage his money. He knew the man's wife and children as well, and, even though there were no hard feelings because the sale had been managed well and Chase had paid a fair price, he still wished he could have helped them save or invest this money more wisely.

The third piece of land was inherited by the brother of one of Chase's best friends in the area, and this brother and his wife were building a house nearby and needed some money to complete their roof. This couple had also been farming the land and were planning to sell it, but with little success. Still, it was located on the ocean, so it had some value. They really needed money for the roof and also to pay the workers who'd built the walls. This piece of land was clearly theirs because no one had disputed it as long as they had been there and farming it. And everyone knew that their father used to live on it and that it had been split between three brothers. Problem was, it didn't show up on the deed for the adjacent plot they owned because the map in the deed showed only ocean. Local government officials hadn't processed any of this family's documents for this land on the ocean because the authorities wanted to be given a portion of it before they would do the paperwork. It is also possible that the officials wanted to keep this coastal land undocumented just in case a rich buyer came in, and they could profit from the sale. They could do by this offering the coastal tract for sale without informing the individuals who actually owned it. This all made for a risky purchase. But Chase liked the piece of land and wanted to help this couple, so he took the risk and bought it after consulting with other friends who lived in the area. He then built a cement and rock fence foundation around the boundary of the land which created a permanent sign to tell everyone that the land had been purchased. There were still no documents proving that Chase owned the land other than a signed receipt listing the amount paid and the plot's location and dimensions. He hoped that a deed for this land would be forthcoming eventually, but he wasn't sure.

These three land purchases each had social and financial situations that made them a little risky, because there is much more to each of these situations that just having the proper paperwork. The financial problem was whether Chase could ever develop the undocumented coastal land from the couple with full confidence that it would not be taken by someone else. The social problem was whether there were options for helping the already poor man who ended up gambling away all the money he received from one of his only land assets. There was also the situation with the woman and whether it would have been better to take advantage of a good price while she was in a difficult situation, or to try and act fairly, leaving her open to later be taken advantage of by someone else. Chase would have had good intentions for the community, but the latter buyer did not have good intentions for the woman and would probably not be a good contributing member of the community in the long run. When trying to act sustainably by making land development decisions with socio-cultural factors in mind, the challenges are manifold.

Analysis

In these matters, one must consider the long-term welfare and development of a community, financial accountability and help for the poor, and the prudence of financial decisions based on relationships without proper documentation. These touch on sustainable tourism practices, with special concern for the sociocultural angles.

Long Term Welfare and Development of a Community

The issue of how to balance making a personal profit and helping the poor during a financial transaction can be a difficult one. As in the first example, Chase even tried to help the woman by giving her more than she was asking for the land. But this eventually led to a worse situation regarding the landholders in the community. It may have helped this woman individually, but it was probably harmful to the community in the long-term. Chase should probably just have tried to get the best deal that he could; then, if he did not need all of the land, he could have given it or sold it to someone with the long-term interests of the community in mind. The important thing would be that Chase was not pressuring the seller to do something she did not want to do in a difficult situation. But if she wanted to bless Chase with more land at a good price because he was helping her out, then he should probably have obliged her and received it as a sign of appreciation. Helping people out in tough situations is powerful.

Financial Accountability and Help for the Poor

The man who was selling his land was in a difficult financial situation, but it was because of some bad decisions he had made in the past. With this history, it is highly likely he would make more bad decisions in the future, but, with a circle of friends around him, this likelihood could be reduced. Even though Chase had coordinated with others in the community to make sure he was in a good place to use this money, as time went on, the seller made another bad decision and lost the money. It might have been possible to phase the payment to help him avoid the temptation of spending it all at once. Perhaps he could have distributed some of it to his wife on a monthly basis to help him lead his family responsibly. These are potentially sensitive moves, especially if there is not a personal relationship between the seller and the buyer. The buyer would have to be careful to offer these options in a respectful way and ensure that the seller did not suspect the buyer of trying to take advantage of him by holding onto the money longer. This brings to mind the fate of American lottery winners who fail to handle their money well; it might be good to offer an option to lump sum distribution. Also, going over the business plan for the chicken farm with the seller and offering helpful suggestions could be beneficial if the basic relationship so allowed.

Financial Decisions Based on Relationships

The waterfront purchase from the couple does have the most important document in a land sale—a signed receipt on a 10,000 IDR *meterai* (seal), which contains the details of what was sold and for how much—though other documentation may not be in place initially, and the culmination of the matter can get tricky. When land being purchased is administratively separated from a larger piece by the Land Department, the process will not get started until the buyer pays for it. This purchase can be risky when the seller will not even allow the buyer to see the actual deed before they pay for the land. This requires the buyer to know other trustworthy people who can verify the owner's right to the land. In some cases, there is no deed, but the elders in the area know the story of the land and are willing to verify it before sub-district authorities. In some cases, the local government officials will not document the land without some type of significant financial contribution to them personally. If the buyer really wants to own the land, he may face a large risk. But he can minimize this by having strong and strategic, mutually-beneficial relationships with others in the area, people who can put pressure on the sellers if they try anything dishonest in the future.

CHAPTER 2

Making Enough and Financial Desperation

Yes, we've worked with some Indonesians for whom money matters seem all-consuming, but American examples also come to mind. And we, ourselves, have had moments when such concerns dominate. Of course, anxiety over money issues is not a sure indicator of spiritual emptiness, for it may well depend on the goals set before them. They may concern lifestyle expectations—choice of restaurants, entertainment choices, level of disposable income, or a family's comfort level. These goals can easily start to feel like real "needs" in life, especially when a spouse, child, or extended family is constantly pressuring the individuals to provide more, especially when the bank is going to seize an asset because loan payments are not being made. As Westerners we have probably felt some level of such desperation in our lives, but I would venture to say that none of us has ever been in a position where we had no financial responsibility except for providing food for our families, and without any assurance we could do that. But this is something I think most Indonesians have dealt with in their lives, and it is hard for us to really relate to that, even though we might think that we can.

An American student who visited us for several months said that he knows what it is like to live without enough money to eat, but I think he was missing a fundamental difference between his situation and that of many Indonesians. He was watching his money very closely and just eating ramen noodles and some cheap hamburgers each day as he worked off of a strict budget, but this was at a time when he was paying thousands of dollars a semester to go to school and had a job providing enough to cover this. But in order to prioritize tuition and rent, he had to watch the amount he spent on food. He was also living out from under his parent's roof for the first time and wanted to prove to himself and others that he could make it on his own. He could have taken a semester off, worked more hours, saved some money and eaten better, but he was familiar with the spiritual benefits of fasting. He also committed himself to toughing it out to get done with school faster. This was commendable, but he was very different from an Indonesian who had nothing to pay off and was just trying to make enough to eat.

Some of these Indonesians also lack real employment options other than starting a small business on their own. And it wasn't just a matter of toughing it out personally; they had wives and kids being forced to fast. This Western student could have also called his parents at any moment, and they would have helped him with money if he really needed it, even though it would be embarrassing for him. Many of these Indonesians would feel the same embarrassment asking for money, but in most cases their family members are in the same financial position as they are and might have even been thinking about asking them for money.

This is the financial desperation that many Indonesians find themselves in when they move to another province for work, and this can affect almost all aspects of their lives. I would guess that most Westerners working overseas make ten to twenty times as much as the average

Indonesian; and we trust 100 percent that our salary will come on time and in the amount we expect. We don't deal with the same financial concerns our national partners do by any stretch of the imagination. Even if we overextend ourselves to cover college expenses for a child or for a home purchase back in the states, these decisions do not impact our actual survival. They're luxuries. And even if we thought that we didn't make enough doing what we're doing overseas, we could quit. We'd likely have our ticket back to the US covered, as well as some months of salary. People and/or churches with plenty of money would help take care of us for a while, and we'd be able to find a job, probably making more than we do now. This is our reality, and this financial security is something we often, unintentionally, take for granted.

A way to avoid this financial desperation in the lives of our Indonesian employees is by making sure that they have enough to live on comfortably, even providing them some financial margin to think about sending their kids to college and buying small pieces of land or life insurance policies to help set their families up for the future and provide for their own retirement. Sometimes I've heard from those I work with that they can't afford meat for their family—only vegetables and rice—or that they're getting on to each other about unplugging their refrigerator for several hours a day to save some money. I need to be sensitive to such needs, especially when I just overhear them talking about these matters. I can't imagine a scenario where I wouldn't have an extra one hundred dollars during the month to help one of my employees in a situation like that. And if I am close to them, I need to be able to tell what is going on without their telling me. And their security should be sustainable, not through episodic welfare payments, but by encouraging and helping them find a way to earn more money through creative enterprise and more work. We need wisdom and experience in how best to provide our employees with more income when they are having trouble making ends meet, but the difficulty of doing this right should never keep me from trying to do it when I see that they are having a hard time. This weighs on me because they are usually doing the same kind of work I'm doing, while I have a guaranteed salary that is ten to twenty times theirs. This is a constant reminder to me of how I have been blessed and how I need to help take care of others who are close to me, but who do not have the same financial resources that I do.

Since our employees guide tourists from the US, I need to be very careful about the way that money comes in and ensure that it is always distributed in an understandable and equitable way. I don't want my employees to start seeing little cracks or opportunities in the way they are paid, angles that would enable them to make more than others, causing an imbalance and leading them to take their focus away from doing their job well. Of course, this concerns their receiving personal financial gifts from the visitors. If guests do want to give an additional large tip, they usually tell me first, and I receive it on behalf of our employees and make sure it is distributed in an equitable way. Smaller personal tips are fine because they are not as visible, and guests usually try to distribute those evenly to all the employees directly.

In many cases, guests ask if tips or gifts are appropriate for people whose houses they visit throughout their trip, and they often ask our employees what amount would be proper. Since the guides are paid sufficiently through their normal means of support, they can be trusted to give advice to guests about giving large sums of money to others who are even more in need. Many of these same guests would give a financial tip or gift to the guides at the end of their tour, but our employees are not trying to work an angle to enlarge that sum by talking about their own needs; adequately-compensated, they can more clearly see the others around them who are more in need. My employees who are believers are also in a position to use their own tithes and offerings to support others in need, because they feel they have been blessed sufficiently to do so (as I do). This is a sign of maturity and an opportunity for them to be used by the Lord, without taking their focus away from work, because they do not live in the financial desperation that so many Indonesians find themselves in.

CHAPTER 3

True Ownership

Because of the nature of our work and legal status within Indonesia, an asset may be in the name of someone who doesn't actually own the asset. For example, if a vehicle is in our name, and we didn't use our personal funds to buy the asset and we can't ethically sell the asset and keep the money to ourselves, then we do not actually own the asset. In the chapter on "Appropriate Financial Responsibility," I get into more detail about salaries and assets that we entrust to employees. But the concept of true ownership of these assets, regardless of whose name they are in, is a different matter. This must take into consideration the initial intent of the purchase or construction, prior agreements, risk assumed, and the actual time and effort spent towards developing the asset by each of the stakeholders. This determines who actually owns the asset, who may make financial decisions regarding it, and who has rights to the money the asset generates if it is sold. As in the movie, *The Social Network*, about the founding of Facebook, it is very important to determine who actually came up with a creative idea for something that is successful, because intellectual property is a real thing. It is also just as important to consider who actually made that idea come to fruition, e.g., by providing the funding, managing the project, and working on it. Those involved in these two fundamental roles should both be considered the owners, though the percentage of ownership they each are due is up for discussion. This arrangement does not need to be fifty-fifty to be fair; it can be weighted in different ways depending upon a variety of factors. The fundamental requirement is that all of the stakeholders involved in these activities related to creating something new agree (or reach an acceptable compromise) on the final decision about ownership.

For example, let's say you have at least one house in the name of an employee, where the employee was the first one to bring up the possibility of buying land because it was offered to him for purchase by a local friend. He didn't have the money available to buy it, but he tossed the idea out to you to see what you thought about it. The reasoning was that, by buying land and possibly building a house on it, you could avoid paying rent year after year with nothing tangible to show for it. You had never thought of this as a possibility until he brought it up. At that point you talked with others in the West, as well as others locally. You got the green light to move forward with it, and decided that it was something you should try, even though it was possible you'd just have a half-built house or shack on the land because of a lack of funding. But it turned out over the following years that it was possible for you to complete the construction on a nice house. Individuals made personal contributions, some NGO funds were available, and a business you managed generated income for the project. And as you were able to move in, the savings on rent could go towards improving and/or building the place.

If the new construction can serve as rental property, the rent money should be paid in accordance with the local rate of a house of similar size and quality, and the person should live in the house for the agreed upon amount of time. So, each party holds up their end of the bargain with the contract, just as would have been the case if you rented a place from another person in your city for two years.

If an organization had decided they were going to fund the building of a house that they wanted to own, then they would need to write up a legal document saying this from the beginning, and they would need to commit to provide enough funds for construction to be completed. If that did not happen, even though individuals in the organization said that rental funds could be used to go towards building a house, then the organization does not own the house. The fundamental requirement would be that the rental funds were in line with how much rent would be paid to stay at another similar place in the city at the going market rate (which is usually about 5% of the total value of a house annually), and the individual renting the house would need to be able to actually live in that house for the period of time outlined in the contract. The one responsible for managing the construction of the house must assume responsibility for ensuring these two conditions were met, which might require receiving rental funds earlier than usual in many cases and assuming the financial and institutional risk of paying with their own funds. Or they might find other funds to get the house in a livable state for the agreed upon period of time if the current amount was not enough. If these requirements were not met, that individual would be the one who needed to answer for it, because he was the one who convinced the logistical personnel in the organization that paying rent money to a place still under construction was a sound decision.

In this case the Indonesian is also a stakeholder in that he was the one who actually came up with the original idea of buying land to build a house, and he was the one who started living there originally and had to take care of ongoing logistical matters on site during construction. His name was also on the line legally for everything, including taxes and building permits. You are a stakeholder because you assumed the most financial risk in the endeavor, putting your reputation and word on the line by deciding to go forward with this. Also, the complexity of this situation probably strained relationships with some of your colleagues and even within in your own family. The organization was also a stakeholder because it was willing to trust your judgment and pay rent towards certain things far in advance, even in cases where the rented space in question was not yet ready to occupy when the contract was signed. But it is important to note that the organization did not commit to build the house, but just to pay an amount in line with the going rate to rent a place for a specified period of time. So, the agreed upon legal requirement regarding the building for the organization was just to have a rented space for that period of time, and not ownership or future free space. In this situation I would argue that the stakeholder with the largest percentage of ownership in this endeavor would be you, as the one assuming most of the risk and being the one most pivotal in making it happen. But this must be tempered by the fact that you would not have been in that location with the time to manage something like that if your organization hadn't made it possible for you to be there.

The Indonesian's role in this was crucial as well, because he was the only one out of the three stakeholders who had the right to legally own the land; all the paperwork needed to be in his name, and he had to be willing to assume legal responsibility for construction and maintenance of the house on a practical level by being the one committed to it long term. By agreeing to have the house in his name, he was in effect saying that he was committed to living and working there long-term, and also that he trusted that you would not legally take advantage of using his name for things that were not in his best interest.

Incidentally, Indonesians are familiar with the concept of being taken advantage of in this way. For instance, it happens when a family member uses a relative's land certificate, BPKB (vehicle ownership deed), or KTP (government identity card) as collateral for a loan. There can be a lot of social pressure from family or employer to do this, and it puts at great risk the one whose ID is being used; if things go south with the investment, he's the one on the spot.

So, in my eyes, the Indonesian, you, and the organization could each be considered as owning about 33.3 percent of this property, which would

be splitting it into thirds for simplicity's sake. But many overseas organizations don't really want to own and be responsible for too many properties,
especially random ones in remote parts of Indonesia where they just have
rights to a portion of the property, and managing it would be considered
more a burden than a benefit. And since there are restrictions on how
foreigners are supposed to benefit from personal property investments in
Indonesia, you might have a hard time claiming your personal right to the
property in court. The Indonesian is mainly thankful that he has a place
to live and work and doesn't know all the details about where the money
came from, so he doesn't really know whether he has rights to any of it
financially. If the Indonesian and you work together for a business, then
it may be best to consider the property an asset of the business, the use
and disposition of which can be decided among the shareholders, and not
just for the financial benefit of any one person. That being said, the two
people in the best position to make decisions regarding the asset are the
two primary local stakeholders—the Indonesian who is currently living in
(or using, or whose name it is in—usually the same person) the asset and
you—because those two have the most invested in the asset regarding time
and risk, and the status of the asset will affect them the most. But since the
presence of the foreigner might still be made possible by an outside organization, I would consider input from the organization to hold significant
weight regarding the asset. True ownership is a complicated issue: They're
local assets managed by local business teams, which are made up of people
from different countries, with different means of financial support, who
have envisioned and executed different parts of the process, all the while
trying to follow the Lord's leading.

Another example concerns land that an Indonesian owned and had
plans for before you entered into a financial relationship with him regarding that asset. Once the rental period is up, these properties would probably return to sole ownership by the Indonesian. Let's say there is land
without a livable house on it, and you used funds to create a livable house
there. It could be there was no house at all and, in accordance with the
amount spent on the construction of the house (compared to current

rental rates), you have the right to use that house for twenty-five years before it returns to the owner, and then he can do what he wants with it. Or, if a house just had a foundation built and a well drilled, and you built ninety-five percent of the house, but it did not cost much to build, you have the right to use that house for ten years.

And then there's the case of a house which was already built and someone could feasibly still live in it, but it had no running water and electricity and it had deteriorated to the point that it could fall down in the coming years. After renovating this house, the money spent on it justified having a fifteen-year contract to use it, after which it would fully return to the owner. I consider the length of time that you're permitted to use these properties to be a fair exchange for the amount of money paid to build or renovate them. A limited period of use is the condition placed on land certificates in the name of foreigners or businesses in Indonesia, because they do not get *Hak Milik* (ownership), but they do get *Hak Guna Bangunan* (HGB, right to use the building) from the Indonesian government. This means that, if this status is not extended beyond the initial time period (usually after fifteen or twenty years), then it returns to the government (or possibly to the person who sold it to the business or foreigner). It is also possible that the foreigner or business could lose their right to the land even if they wanted to retain it, because they did not actually own it. These businesses and foreigners need to decide if building a property and being able to use it for twenty years is going to be worth it for them. And if they decide to pursue HGB, then they have decided it is.

CHAPTER 4

Social Entrepreneurship and Sustainability

This is as much a confession as it is a prescription. Westerners moving overseas to places like Indonesia are usually more concerned with not getting ripped off in our interactions with locals, than with trying to benefit those around us financially. Most of us would probably respond with, "Of course, we just want to be treated fairly." But having too much of a concern with "fairness" can sometimes keep us from doing the best for others. I started to realize this after a minor traffic accident in Indonesia. I was turning into my driveway, had signaled about fifty feet in advance, and had checked my mirrors. Then, all of a sudden, a motorcycle seemed to come out of nowhere, trying to pass me, but, when he saw that I was halfway through the turn, he slammed on his brakes, and his motorcycle went down. He slid about ten feet, seemed to be okay, stood up, and walked over to my window. I was ready to make sure he knew that he was in the wrong, but he immediately admitted that he had been wrong. Then he said that he didn't have enough money to replace his sideview mirror and fix a bent foot peg, so he asked if he could have the equivalent of five dollars from me to help with that. My first thought was that I shouldn't pay this guy anything; the fact that he went down was totally his fault. But then I started to think, "Why wouldn't I help this guy out with five dollars?"

It's true that I could easily part with that amount of money, and it would help this guy out with a need. The goal in the aftermath of many traffic incidents in Indonesia is not just to determine who was right or wrong, but how the situation can be resolved. The authorities are rarely involved, unless it's really serious, because they usually just make the situation more complicated. No one has insurance, so it often comes down to what's worked out at the scene. You usually need to come out of the car ready to defend your case, but these light altercations are often a chance to act with understanding. If we hold too tightly to a guiding principle about who is right and wrong in all situations, we can end up just being stingy and uncaring. Sure, we risk being taken advantage of, but is that really the worst risk we could take? Wouldn't it be better to hazard that, than to risk not helping someone who was really in need when it was in our power to do so? We don't need more practice in looking out for ourselves, but if we had eyes to see the situation aright, we could use opportunities like these to risk being too generous.

Books like *When Helping Hurts* are very good in leading us to think how to be most effective in assisting others. The authors believed "that when North American Christians do attempt to alleviate poverty, the methods used often do considerable harm to both the materially poor and the materially non-poor."[46] There have also been books written on how things can go wrong with financial matters overseas. I won't spend much time here focusing on how things can go wrong, but more on things that I have done or observed that seem to have gone right after fifteen years. I do try to address how often the decisions we make regarding finances can set up those we work with for success, as opposed to putting an obstacle in their path, a barrier making it difficult for them to act with integrity. As Westerners, we are susceptible to very similar temptations, but their scale and framing can blind us to their semblance. Of course, concern over the prospect of doing more harm than good should always be on our minds, but not to the point that it paralyzes us.

We can also have too many contracts and written documents in place to make us feel more secure in business dealings overseas, while in many cases these documents can cause suspicion and are not really worth the paper they are printed on if our relationships go sideways. We need to be experts in dealing with others on a personal level and ensure that we are transparent, straightforward, and clear, especially in situations prone to misunderstanding. But the bottom line is that we should do what we can to mitigate the risk in an appropriate way, through a variety of social means, and then go all in on supporting those we believe in, while having the same patience and understanding with them that we would hope we would receive from others.

I think that in Western societies today, the pendulum has swung too far in the direction of being overly cautious in our dealing with believers overseas, and this has unconsciously become a way to feel we are off the hook when it comes to difficult and complicated issues in helping others overseas. I'm reminded of one of the first things repeated over and over to me when I first moved overseas, counsel regarding helping beggars at stoplights. It's said that, in Indonesia, many of the ladies at stoplights holding little children and asking for money have just rented (or borrowed) those kids for the day so that they look needier than they really are. Because of that possibility, we were told we shouldn't help them because it would just encourage them to continue begging in a deceptive way. So, we rarely give money to beggars at stoplights, and we almost felt righteous about it because we knew we aren't being taken advantage of. But in reality, there's nothing righteous about not helping others in need. The better question is, "How can we best help those in need?" But in order for us to really be able to answer this question, I would suggest that we need to loosen our grip a little on a principle we most assuredly all have concerning the question, "Do they really deserve my help?"

In Khalil Gibran's popular work, *The Prophet*, he attempts to frame a way we could start to think about giving. He writes,

> All you have shall some day be given;
> Therefore, give now, that the season of giving may be yours and not your inheritors'.
> You often say, "I would give, but only to the deserving."
> The trees in your orchard say not so, nor the flocks in your pasture.
> They give that they may live, for to withhold is to perish.
> Surely, he who is worthy to receive his days and his nights, is worthy of all else from you.
> And he who has deserved to drink from the ocean of life deserves to fill his cup from your little stream.
> And who are you that men should rend their bosom and unveil their pride, that you may see their worth naked and their pride unabashed?
> See first that you yourself deserve to be a giver, and an instrument of giving.[47]

There is wisdom in not encouraging beggars to keep begging, but it's hard to know if our inaction is actually leading them in that direction. A quick way to help them if we wanted to would be to hand out water or food, which we know they need, and, as a non-cash gift, it wouldn't be spent on renting someone else's child, on alcohol, or on drugs. But the best solution would be to help them in a long-term way, so that they would no longer feel they needed to beg. This is the complicated issue this book attempts to address. And while it doesn't focus on helping beggars, but more on those who are close to us and we can depend on, I hope the type of thinking illustrated in this book can impact all areas of our lives and our interactions with others. Doing what we can to help others overseas in the manner I am suggesting relates to two concepts that we often hear today—social entrepreneurship and sustainability.

Social entrepreneurship is a for-profit business model that strives to make a positive impact on community issues or the environment. So, a social entrepreneur is a person who explores business opportunities that have a positive impact on the world. Some of the more well-known corporate examples are TOMS, Warby Parker, FIGS, Love Your Melon, and Lush. These businesses do such things as give a pair of shoes to poor children for each pair purchased, donate glasses and related vision care to underprivileged children around the world, and support animal welfare.[48] For these companies, making money is still a priority, but making a difference socially is also a big part of what they do. On a much smaller scale in Eastern Indonesia, this is what I have tried to do.

In order to truly be a long-term solution for the partners I work with in Indonesia, the business needs to be sustainable. Business sustainability is usually understood to have a "triple bottom line" (not just the economic bottom line of profit and loss), of social well-being, environmental health, and a just economy. Or more simply put: people, planet, and profit.[49] I will be focusing more on social well-being, while also spending a good amount of time on the most foundational of the three, a just economy. As for our work abroad through small scale tourism, our positive impact on the environment is pretty much limited to putting our trash in the right place, helping clean up the trash of others, and ensuring that any waste we produce is disposed of properly. When it comes to the economic and social aspects of sustaining a small business in remote area, the task is more complicated, calling for more than money and a proper education. For the way we work with, and view, others cross-culturally is critical.

I want to remind entrepreneurs that business efforts in remote places usually need to start small, and the focus on people would first of all be directed toward the handful of employees you have. Sustainability in these situations is about being able to support yourself and the employees you work with for the long-term through the business you have established. This is different from the ESG (Environmental, Social, and Government) criteria used by larger companies to screen potential investments or to effect some type of change in others. This social entrepreneurship is much more personal. It's about carefully choosing individuals whom you can rely on, who also believe they can rely on you. These must be friends who share a certain level of mutual understanding about what you all want to accomplish, and those to whom you would be comfortable deferring in difficult decisions. These need to be individuals you would make sacrifices for, and you know they would be willing to do the same for you. This is not about accomplishing political goals or influencing a society; this is about taking care of those on your right and your left in the same foxhole, to use a military analogy.

Another Westerner living overseas argues in his book, *No Shortcut to Success*, that we need to study the language and culture for many years, and take it slow, because it's essential to communicate clearly and effectively with those they want to impact with the gospel.[50] Studying language and culture are very important, but not because everything relies upon us down to the most remote and undeveloped areas. This common mindset is an outgrowth of the autonomy and independence that we are so proud of in America. I agree with Rhodes that we should push back against the impatient and detached nature of American culture today, and make long-term commitments overseas, but the most efficient, effective (and biblical) way to achieve success overseas is to invest our lives in other believers who share our values. There is still some Western impatience reflected in the resolve, "If this is going to be done, I just need to do it myself." But there are more believers and Bible translations throughout the most unreached countries of the world today than ever before. There are thousands of believers in each of these countries with whom we could partner in some way to accomplish change that is more sustainable long-term, if, that is, we would be more patient in our relationships with other Christians. Even though it's hard to work together with others when we want to do things on our own or have a hard time listening to and observing things outside of what we think is best, it is worth the effort. Rhodes gives a nod to these challenges in his book, but I think we need to press harder on how to partner well overseas instead of relegating these relationships with national partners as a sideshow to our primary work because of possible complications.[51] I have seen too many social entrepreneurs try to "start from scratch" in the places they live instead of relying on local partners to help them in areas where they are weak. Overseas, this usually ends in disappointment and short-lived-ventures.

The principles at the end of this book are meant to help us all deal with heart issues concerning who is worthy to receive help and how to get along well with others, using Scripture as our guide. It should help us step back from some of the core principles of independence and self-reliance we have as Westerners and see if they should really always be our guide when helping others overseas. In many cases, as the Seven Levels explain, we are less worthy as guides than we think we are. Only when we start to see ourselves clearly can we start to help others who are from a context much different from ours. The next few chapters offer more on the nature and contexts of the communities I work with.

CHAPTER 5

The Faith Community in Needle Rock

In Eastern Indonesia, there is a small community of evangelical Unteli believers who are the local remnant of a movement of God about 85 years ago. Some of the elderly members of this church were little children when this community was still thriving. But that was a long time ago, and a lot has happened since then. This church is small enough to demonstrate what body life might be like for a small house church in Indonesia after two generations. These believers have been part of a traditional Christian-background community for over a generation (about 40 years), and the first generation of converts lived under the authority of an Islamic government (in the late 1930's), ruled by the Sultan of Aroma. (And, yes, the current body still lives in a Muslim majority area and the members have many Muslims who are part of their extended families.) Along with holding regular, traditional worship services, they're attempting to reestablish the Christian community that once lived in the village of Needle Rock. Providentially, a road was built to this attractive area about ten years ago. These Christians have a historical claim to this land, a fact which admirably positions them to be a long-term light for Christ on the island.

A large portion of the village of Nantas on the coast of the island of Unteli came to faith in the 1930s, the result of the witness of some Torajanese believers associated with an evangelical church in Makassar. A key factor was the way in which some of the stories about Jesus lined up with things foretold about the future of the village by an elder in the community. Since the lifestyle of these new believers contrasted with that of those around them, they eventually moved a few miles away to start their own community, ending up across a narrow strait on the coast of a neighboring island. They built a village and church building there, but after about forty years, a large wave created by a falling rock the size of a football field from Unteli wiped out most of the houses in the village. Some people died, but most of the people survived because they were working their farmland, farther inland. At that point in the early 1970s, most of these believers decided to move far away to the Spice Islands, where there were more Christians and they already had some connections. Most of the people from this original Christian community still live in the Spice Islands today, but some of them returned to their home island during the violent conflict there around the year 2000. Some from this Needle Rock Christian community returned to their original land on the north side of the city of Aroma, while some established a community on the east side of the island, just north of Market city. Others blended with the local population and began worshiping at various other churches on the west side of their island.

When we arrived in Aroma in 2007, we started looking around at local churches and were told that most of them were made up of people from Christian-background people groups from other provinces, but that there was one indigenous church that no longer met in Aroma. There was really only one baptistic church locally, and, since it was primarily made up of one of the indigenous people groups, we sought out someone who knew about it. We found Mr. Story and his wife Mrs. Story and decided to start worshiping together in Aroma, and a *Pos Penginjilan* (Pos PI, or Preaching point, like a church plant) was eventually started. After worshiping together for about ten years, sometimes with a college intern as a pastor and sometimes not, this *Pos PI* became an official church, named Ebenezer. But the foundational "rock of remembrance" for this Christian community was found in the village of Needle Rock, farther north, but still considered part of the city of Aroma. Then in 2021, regular worship for this church was moved to Needle Rock on the property of the original church, and the name was changed to "Needle Rock of Remembrance." We have been living life along with this local body of believers, made up of about ten heads of family, for about fifteen years.

There are advantages and disadvantages to working with small, traditional Christian churches, and they can also offer a glimpse into what a house church may eventually look like long-term. Being involved with this small Christian community in the religious minority has made for an informative journey, and I hope it has contributed to a long term, positive Christian presence among the people where we live. The church has relied upon what the Lord did many years ago among the Unteli people, long before I was born, and it's still here. But it's not pretty, and I don't think the Lord expects it to be. Many people talk about the messiness of church planting, but details are rarely shared about how this messiness is an aspect of all churches in this fallen world, congregations containing sinful people. In this picture of the Needle Rock church, I'll provide a brief background and character description of each of the ten heads of family, some key efforts the church has been involved in, worship habits, and shortcomings, as well as significant events and challenges that have shaped the life of the church over the past fifteen years.

Members

1. **Mr. and Mrs. Story**—They have four grown children, two of which were still in junior high and high school when this Needle Rock church started meeting again. Mr. Story is the oldest resi-

dent member of the church and the one most pivotal in getting it started again. He also knows the story of all the land in Needle Rock, and has been pivotal in the process of claiming the land for individuals from Needle Rock while outsiders try to take it over. He says that his father called Needle Rock their promised land, or "Canaan." He feels this land was given to them by the Lord for a reason, and they should steward it well. A goat farm now rests on the land where he grew up, and he is preparing plots and makeshift houses for each of his children in Needle Rock. He also farms. He was a key part of a Story Together project for the Unteli language, with him and his wife translating some other Unteli evangelism and discipleship materials. He is also well respected by Muslims in the area and is seen as one of the main leaders of the Needle Rock community. His wife was a teacher, retiring in 2019. He is also the commissioner of the goat farm business. He had a stroke in early 2023 and now has a hard time getting around.

2. **Mr. and Mrs. Farmer**—Mr. Farmer is Mr. Story's younger brother. He drove a dump truck for many years and also had a chronic drinking problem. He married a formerly-Muslim woman after she became pregnant out of wedlock, but she has turned out to be more dedicated to studying the Bible than he has. Both of them were discipled for a couple of years by an Indonesian friend before they started going to church again. They have five children, all them still in school. The three oldest are from Mrs. Farmer's previous marriages to Muslim men, whom she later divorced. The Farmers have lived physically in Needle Rock longer than anyone else and have built the first personally-owned brick house there (other than the goat farm). They've led out in keeping the goats fed and milked for the past ten years. They've taken part in Bible studies in the past and attend worship regularly, but they're not comfortable praying out loud, and they rarely contribute to spiritual discussions. The details and extent of their spiritual relation-

ship with the Lord are not very clear, but they are faithful and important members of this community.

3. **Mr. and Mrs. Business**—Mr. Business is the head of the church's *majelis* (elders) and is a local businessman who cooks and sells bread throughout the city of Aroma. He has been successful with this and has also been involved with several multi-level marketing businesses in the past, along with other members of this community. Most of those didn't work out very well. Mr. Business is a passionate guy, who often leads worship and has made speeches in the past about the importance of evangelism and the church's making headway in this area. He's expressed frustration over his inability to find the right words to share his faith effectively, but he would like to go along with believers who do well at this and give his support. He is bold in telling people they need to surrender to Christ and come to church, but has a hard time sharing his faith with those who have yet to believe. His heart seems to be in the right place and he is an important part of this community, especially for those who are a generation younger than Mr. Story.

4. **Mr. and Mrs. Network**—Mr. Network is Mr. Business's younger brother, and when we first started with this community, he would often preach. He's always a friendly, funny, and talkative guy who is knowledgeable of Scripture. He was one of the only members of this church who would actually go out and share his faith after attending T4T (Training for Trainers) about fifteen years ago. I think the older generation hoped he would one day become a pastor, but he fell in love with the girl across the street in Needle Rock, and she ended up getting pregnant out of wedlock, and they were married. Mrs. Network has been difficult to deal with for everyone at many times, and at one point it seemed as though she wanted to derail any hope of formal ministry in Mr. Network's life. But in recent years she has grown spiritually, better able to balance the pressures of life. They now go to another church, but he is still involved with this Needle Rock community, and he is a

strong evangelist and disciple-maker. He is also a great tour guide, and he is constantly working through the details of how to balance work with ministry and make enough to support his family. He's talented musically, can speak English pretty well, and is comfortable in remote areas.

5. **Mr. Grain**—Mr. Grain is married with children, but his wife is in the Spice Islands, and Mr. Grain stays in Needle Rock. He really cares about this community and is from the same generation as Mr. Story. He is a retired civil servant, doing some farming and trying to make sure his land is taken care of. He goes back to the Spice Islands regularly and is the assistant commissioner of the goat farm business.

6. **Mr. and Mrs. Coconut**—Mr. Coconut is Mr. Grain's oldest son. He and his family live on the other side of the island with the Needle Rock community near Market City. They often come to worship with us in Needle Rock because we all know them well, and Mr. Grain likes to spend time with his grandson. Mrs. Coconut did a ministry internship with the *Pos PI* (preaching point) in Bones back around 2013. After she graduated from Bible school in Makassar, she ended up getting married to Mr. Coconut and moved to the island. They have one son.

7. **Mr. and Mrs. Guard**—Mr. Guard attends off and on, but often has financial and drinking problems. His wife is usually there, but doesn't say much. They have two children who are in junior high and high school. They usually live in a warehouse or a small place they guard for the person who owns it. Not sure of the spiritual state of these two. PS: In 2022, Mrs. Guard was found dead out in a field with coconut trees, and no one knows exactly what happened.

8. **Mr. Motor**—Mr. Motor used to be married when he lived in the Spice Islands, but he seems to have gotten divorced. He is the main one who delivered goat milk for many years, and he did odd jobs with the farm. Now he primarily manages parking spaces at the Needle Rock tourist site for an older local lady. He usually

comes to worship and has attended Bible study in the past, but I haven't heard him discuss anything spiritual. He's not talkative but is a nice guy.

9. **Mr. Uncle**—Mr. Uncle is in the same generation as Mr. Story and Mr. Farmer, so he's an older guy. It's tough to really have a conversation with him, though he'll have intermittent bursts of talking. He feels that Needle Rock has been blessed by God, but I haven't seen much spiritual fruit in his life. He is a pretty nice guy who does odd jobs at the goat farm, like gathering feed and cleaning pens. He also fishes, dries and sells seaweed, and does other random things around Needle Rock. He was married to a Christian lady who lives in the Spice Islands, but they have been separated for many years. The church will not give him an official letter to finalize a divorce, so he married a local Muslim lady and lives with her in Needle Rock. He is still a part of the Needle Rock community, though is in a tenuous position religiously because of his marriages.

10. **Mr. Carpenter**—Mr. Carpenter is a pretty talented single guy in his 40s who has never been married. He is working little by little on a brick house on the other side of the goat farm from Mr. Farmer's house. Having built Mr. Farmer's house, he's shown that he's good at construction, and he's the one leading the reconstruction of the church building. He has also led in drama productions at the church in the past, leads the group of young people at the church, and usually plays guitar during worship. He is respected by the churches in the Spice Islands, and he played a key role when over a hundred believers from those islands came back with their children to Needle Rock in 2016 to put on a Christmas service so their kids could see where they came from.

Community Efforts

We met for about five years in the house of Mr. Story in Bones, but the pastor (or college intern from Makassar) always needed to live with Mr. Story, and the place where the worship was held could not always accommodate everyone; it was tough for everyone to see the person preaching because the members were sitting in different rooms. They eventually built worship space a short walk up a hill from Mr. Story's house in Bones, on church land, with funds from their congregation and from wealthy denomination members from other, larger cities on a bigger island.

The government granted permission to build this building as a parsonage, but it also served as a place of worship. All the churches in town built in the last forty years have needed to be creative with permissions, with requests for multi-purpose or event buildings, since churches have not been successful recently in getting enough signatures from the neighbors to designate it a house of worship. In this vein and generally speaking, the local government officials delay church paperwork for years to the extent they have power to do so. They have been very successful at this in Aroma, knowing that a church building is often one of the requirements for a church to move from preaching-point status to an official-church standing.

Another important requirement for the long-term health of a church is dedicated leadership. This church has had six month-to-one-year interns from a Bible college. They needed to have some practical experience to finish their degrees, so they were placed in our church to help with leadership. The more effective interns seemed to integrate better with the young people in the church and outside of it, and they were able to take trips out to more remote areas with local friends for ministry. These young interns had a hard time claiming the same status as the older pastors in other churches, but they were able to exert some pastoral leadership depending on the individual. Either way, when the intern left, the church would often go back to how was, once again being led by the elders through cooperation within this congregation with no dedicated pastor. In early 2021, the church had its first permanent pastor (originally from Borneo) appointed after he graduated from Bible school, and he ended up marrying Mr. Business and Mr. Network's sister. So, we are looking forward to some stability from Pastor Shepherd and his wife Mrs. Shepherd.

An effort is also underway to rebuild the original church building in Needle Rock, working from the foundation, a wall, and several pillars that remain from the 1960s. But it's taken about five years to even get the deed processed, showing legally that this was church land. All of the nearby local villages and leaders in those villages knew this was a church building and church land from a long time ago, but the local government officials seemed to feel it was their job to delay and obstruct the administration of this deed. They said it was government land because no one worshipped there anymore. Even so, the deed was finally completed in the church's name, and eventually construction began to rebuild as funds became available. Many of these funds were from outside donors because the local community was only able to fund the building where they worshipped weekly in Bones, even though this was an important building for the future of the Needle Rock community.

After many years of partial improvement, intermixed with verbal comments from officials saying it shouldn't be rebuilt because it didn't have recent permission, the believers called a meeting with the leaders of the nearby village and sub-district to garner support for the rebuilding of the church. Everyone who attended agreed (about thirty people), but the head of the sub-district would not sign the letter saying that this meeting happened. She probably thought she would get in trouble, or she wanted personal compensation. After the pastor and several of the church leaders met with the head of the district and the mayor to request permission to rebuild this historic church, they were eventually given a letter saying they needed to get ninety signatures from believing "users" of the church building and sixty signatures from non-believing members of the local community saying they supported this church building in order—all this for the permission to even be processed. Each of these signatures had to be accompanied by a KTP (national ID) number for the individual.

This signature process was underway for over a year, with the ninety signatures being garnered from a variety of believers throughout the city of Aroma, people who would worship there at least once a year at Christmas time, and there were about forty signatures from local Muslims who supported this building. But then announcements were made at some of the local mosques that Muslims should not sign this paper, so the campaign stalled out short of the required signatures. Even Muslim men who had previously said they would sign it apologized saying they couldn't, or they would get in trouble. There was some pressure nationally to end this signature requirement, because it had been used to discriminate against non-Muslim religions for several years. Maybe because of this pressure, the local committee that is supposed to help with these matters had one of its members say the church should just start building slowly and maybe try to register it as a multi-purpose building. The community had originally hoped this church building would be grandfathered in as already permitted (as it should have been) because of how old it was, but local officials were more interested in making it difficult. In the meantime, an Islamic school was started in this Christian community and a mosque was built within a year without asking the Christians who lived there anything about this.

There have been steady and ongoing efforts for nearby Muslim locals to claim the land in the Needle Rock area because it is a strategic area, and most of the believers from this community have lived in the Spice Islands for many years, and only a few come to visit regularly. The believers who live locally have been the ones playing a very important role in preserving this historic village. They know the story of the village, who lived where and who owns what, but they don't really have extra money to put into reclaiming and redeveloping this village. Many of the wealthy Muslims in the nearby villages do, and at least one of them said many years ago that they were going to take over Needle Rock because all that the Christians had out there were little shacks. And all along, the government leaders were supporting Muslim efforts.

Around that time, Mr. Story and I were talking about his possibly starting a milk goat farm in Needle Rock, and, when we started building and providing jobs in Needle Rock for the believers, Mr. Story said he never heard anyone in Nutmeg (nearby village) challenge the place of believers in Needle Rock again. No one else was brave enough to put rocks and cement on the ground in Needle Rock, so the believers associated with the goat farm were seen as the true residents and guardians of the Christian community there. Over the following years, we found personally that a good way for our tithe to be used was to pay local believers a fair price for land they wanted to sell, but keep the land in their name for general use for the community. This kept the land from being sold to outsiders, and it gave the local believers money to build wooden houses and start little business efforts in Needle Rock while preserving the land for the community in the future. It was a long-term investment in the community as land here almost always appreciates in value.

In 2016, there was a big Christmas event named "Needle Rock Calling You Home." It was supposed to be one of the first steps in a movement of older believers who were retiring from the Spice Islands to return to the land they had come from to rebuild their old village. It was a pretty cool event, and corporate knowledge of this long-ago Christian community was being revived around the city of Aroma. A lot of people supported it; and many local Muslims attended the event as well. Unfortunately, only a few people from the Spice Islands have come intermittently to administratively process their land. This area continues to be reestablished primarily by those from this community who still live in Aroma. The local government officials say that if everyone from the Spice Islands would return (thousands of people), then the church permission process could be processed easier, but the people in the Spice Islands have been there for a generation, and it is tough to pull up roots and move to a somewhat remote area. There is still an ongoing relationship with the believers in the Spice Islands that ebbs and flows, but it is clear that our local church will be the one to establish a long-term presence for this community starting now, or it will disappear.

A new believer once lived out in Needle Rock and helped with the goat farm, which proved to be a revealing and challenging time for this community and this new believer. This church's denomination is evangelical and often talks about the importance of sharing their faith with unbelievers, and some of the pastors and members have been a part of "mission trips" to more remote areas surrounding the Spice Islands and

Makassar, usually to play the *Jesus Film* or something like that. But when it comes to actually sharing their faith with Muslims close to where they live, this is a big challenge, and I know only two members of this Needle Rock community on the island who are engaged in doing this. Even so, I would venture to say that the percentage of people sharing their faith with locals is higher in this particular church than in the other local churches. The lack of evangelism by traditional Indonesian church members is well known, but when this new believer was integrated into the Needle Rock community, we saw an even deeper problem, an unhealthy discipleship environment for new believers.

This new believer was living on the goat farm in Needle Rock, and while there was some surface acceptance and friendliness between him and the Christian community, there arose ongoing misunderstandings and offenses. The root seems to have been a sense of jealousy on the part of believers because the new believer was good at sharing his faith and the Lord was working in his life, but he was from a different cultural background. Some felt that he was encroaching on their territory, possibly with evil intent. This new believer was still immature in his faith, even though the Lord was clearly at work in his life, so he began to blame others for any shortcomings occurring on the farm in order to make them look worse and himself look better. One of our friends was doing ongoing discipleship with this new believer twice a week, but the local Christian community seemed to only have a negative influence. None of them really knew what it was like to disciple someone else; they were also unsure about how to interact with a former Muslim (and whether he was still a "wolf in sheep's clothing"); so they never took the lead in accepting him into their community.

The new believer grew a lot through these experiences and the ongoing discipleship by our friend, but some bitterness arose in his heart, and especially his wife's. It remains to this day to a certain extent as they have moved back to their home village on Unteli. I think the Needle Rock community is kind of relieved to not have him around, and I am not sure if they realize how this experience exposed the power of culture and self-interest that often dominates their community rather than the gospel and a spirit of self-sacrifice. This new believer is experiencing even more stress back among the Muslim-majority area of his wife's family, and is probably causing stress of his own. So, no matter where we are, we still need to learn to live in humility and understanding of others, even when they hurt or offend us. We would want them to do the same for us.

I consider it a true blessing to be a part of this community and what the Lord is doing among them in spite of all these weaknesses we have as a church body. I see it as representative of the trajectory Indonesian church plants will follow in the future and am trying to glean as much insight as possible from this community where I worship and with whose believers I often work. There are very real institutional frameworks and legal require-ments needed for house churches and their members, which require a long-term frame of mind to guard what's been entrusted to them. These are very reasonable concerns which should not be seen as negatives when put in their proper place.

Of course, there are also habits and mindsets that have developed in traditional churches, things antithetical to the gospel, a reflection of the sinfulness of our humanity and the way that most human institutions will develop over time. These tendencies should not be ignored, because no matter how ideal a church's beginnings, things will probably begin to shift in this direction over time. In addition to working with existing churches to become more healthy, cross-cultural workers should learn lessons from traditional churches about the importance of ongoing, institutionalized, and rigorous discipleship from the beginning. It undergirds the encour-agement and development of church leaders who are called by God so as to keep a church on the correct course long term. None of these efforts is simple and fast; they require time, dedication, and the fostering of deep, personal relationships between believers who are willing to be vulnerable and learn from one another.

Dilemma: Current Church Leadership and Direction Scenario

Since we first moved here, this Christian community has lacked consistent leadership, though there have been several periods when temporary leadership was provided by student interns and short-term pastors assigned from the outside. A similar congregation on the other side of the island has an official full-status pastor, but he is usually more concerned with outside agricultural and development projects than in actually leading the congregation and the believers on this island in a certain direction. The lack of professional pastoral leadership is something that is often touted as positive and organic within house churches, even though these churches should have a pastor. But unless someone sees their main purpose and calling to be a pastor within that community, the church often flails about. From our experience in Needle Rock, we see that a good pastor is difficult to come by. This community of believers continues to stay together, hold worship services, and meet the minimum requirements of a church while lacking a called and trained pastor who is dedicated to the congregation, but it just seems to keep the status quo, with great difficulty in growing and developing. Most of the pastors assigned by the denomination have been singles, who are not very promising for long-term, solid leadership in this predominantly Muslim area, but it is promising that the most recent pastor married a local lady. It is hard to draw a pastor with a family from another area to lead a small congregation in a remote area not able to provide much income, with less than optimal education options for the children. Few pastors want to move here, and the locals in the church don't really feel called to pastor or even know how. What can be done about this?

Economic Challenges to Long-Term Viability

More outsiders are moving into the Needle Rock community with more money and Islamic motivation as the area becomes more developed. Many of these outsiders feel it is their role to not only be in a better position to make a profit on this historically Christian land, but to also reduce the visibility of Christianity and raise the visibility and influence of Islam in this area. It is a small picture of Muslims' trying to dominate an area in religious ways, a phenomenon occurring on a larger scale in places like Papua, North Sulawesi and the Malukus. Is it important for members of historically Christian villages to invest their own money and seek Christian investment into their area for the long-term viability of their community, especially when it directly affects their ability to build and maintain a Christian place of worship? Or are all these pursuits purely worldly, and should they just be content with their lot as farmers, allow more wealthy Muslims to come in, buy their land, and start to build mosques so that there is no visible remnant of Christianity remaining? Is this the more spiritual thing to do, and a true sign of reliance on and trust in God during difficult times? Or is it possible that the Lord would want people to invest their money, time, and abilities in order to preserve villages and areas where Christians can live in community and worship more freely in the future, even if the community is still small?

This situation in Needle Rock is unique, but it has similarities with what's happening in other majority-Christian parts of Indonesia, where many of these majorities are declining because of large amounts of money being put towards the advance of Islam in these areas. Money is often seen as something that corrupts situations when it comes to the advance or preservation of Christianity, but when individuals contribute money, it is also a sign that they actually care about something and believe in it as a cause. NGOs are often notorious wasters of money because they spend other people's money and do not have a personal interest in making a profit in their projects. Individuals who have money personally invested in businesses and churches often care more about what happens in projects because it is their money that risks being lost. How much of our money are we personally investing and risking in our work overseas for the good of the local churches we work with, and how does that reflect our commitment to the Indonesian church and our willingness to sacrifice what we consider ours towards others who are less fortunate, and to what the Lord has called all believers to do?

CHAPTER 6

The Indonesian Church and Westerners

Many of us have been involved with or heard of Indonesian churches wherein prominent members are living in open sin or even pastors who have used their position to do evil and negatively influence others. Of course, the same occurs in American churches, but most of us would never knowingly join a fellowship with leaders like that. We'd want to be a part of a church where we could see ourselves accountable as members of the Body of Christ, grow in the Lord, and pay at least a tithe to support it. In Indonesia, because of cultural and language differences, sometimes it is difficult to find churches that play this type of role in our lives. We might find ourselves in community with a group of people that we come to find are "lost sheep" that need to be saved, not a congregation we believe God can use in our lives "as iron sharpens iron." If we decide we need to redeem the "church" with our own righteousness and teaching, we will probably have a very frustrating experience. Just like unintentionally marrying someone who turns out to be an unbeliever, we will probably bear the consequences of our decision through many difficult circumstances and disappointments. If you do find yourself in that situation, though, this is not always an excuse for you to personally be unfaithful, uncommitted to that assembly. It's somewhat analogous to the case of the Christian who married an unbeliever, or a very sinful "believer." It may be best to try to win them over by submitting yourself to them and showing the love of the Lord (1 Pt 3:1-2). The Lord may be using that situation to teach you to depend on Him and let Him bring about what others intend for evil to accomplish good, and to allow your weakness to show His strength. Regardless of what a person in this situation decides to do, I'm sure we would all agree that this is not the ideal for the life of a believer. We should also not let a very realistic situation like this negatively taint our view of the church or become a stereotype in our mind of all Indonesian churches.

A common pitfall for churchgoers is the practice of jumping from church to church because they are no longer "being fed" or it doesn't do what they say as they use it primarily to get things they want. They join pridefully, and when the church doesn't measure up to their preferences, they leave and try to find another. It's called "church hopping," very short on commitment. When things don't go the way they want, they leave and often miss out on what the Lord could teach them, and also what the Lord could do through them in the life of that church. Again, we might think of marriage: Many suppose it's about loving each other in the context of feeling loved and cared for, and, when that "love" feeling disappears, they are free to leave the marriage and "hop" to another.

Marriage and the church are two very powerful tools the Lord uses to make us more like Christ, and the commitment level should be high. They are not primarily for our pleasure, but to help make us holy. Because of what we will go through in each of these "institutions," it is vitally important that we choose a spouse and a church to which we are committed and for which we are willing to sacrifice a large part of ourselves. Of course, if we make commitments to the wrong spouse or church, we will miss out on so much, and it could play a part in wrecking our lives and the lives of others. So, we must earnestly seek the leading of the Lord in these decisions. But even so, it is easy for foreigners to get into tough situations with Indonesian churches. It is risky to put ourselves in the service to what our spouse or church thinks is important. At times it will require submitting ourselves to decisions of both our spouse and our church that we don't agree with because we are committed to them. Our posture in these situations should not be to maintain bitterness and judge them with ongoing disgruntlement, if, that is, we really want to be in a position for the Lord to achieve what He wants to in our lives and in their lives. If we have a negative stereotype of the Indonesian church, it can turn us into church hoppers, and we can also influence others to do the same.

All of these very real, and bad, situations and stereotypes of Indonesian churches are obstacles for Westerners wishing to associate with local believers. In sum, we must be vigilant regarding the decision on what church we want to be a part of in Indonesia, and if we find a good one, we should not take it for granted and treat it lightly. We should make the most of it; we've not come to Indonesia to live our lives apart from Indonesian churches, but to be a part of a local body of believers just like as if we were in America. Recall how Paul usually started his ministry in a new city at a local synagogue because of some level of commonality. Similarly, we should not ignore or waste the commonality we already have with other believers where we live. It should not be a stretch for us to consider Indonesian believers as brothers in sisters in Christ just as we would fellow Western believers. And if we see them as inferior Christians, this might stem from a heart issue on our part, from our own inability to see clearly because of cross-cultural issues.

This does not mean that when we choose to associate with a church overseas, we overlook important issues such as their stance on baptism and salvation, because many biblical issues are important to adhere to regardless of the culture we find ourself in. But in our daily interaction with other brothers and sisters in Christ in a remote area, we should lean towards showing charity and love to other brothers and sisters in Christ, because most laymen in areas like these haven't really developed a theological position on issues like these and are just following the lead of their parents before them. They feel an affinity with Christians from other countries who come to visit their island, and we should encourage them in their faith, while always being ready to explain the biblical position on deeper issues if the opportunity presents itself. Living as a Christian minority for a long period of time helps one appreciate the importance of fostering community where one can.

Local Indonesians do not need to change just to please us, and we should not assume a judgmental posture over the local church that we choose to be a part of in Indonesia. When we choose it, our default position should be one of respect for and accountability toward that body. If we don't get what we want, we shouldn't write them off presumptuously, calling them "lazy," "dead spiritually," or "disobedient." If that dominates our thoughts in the church that we have chosen to be a part of, we show forth a church-hopper mentality, just being a part of the church because of our own priorities, not as a place that we should submit so that God can use it as a tool to make us and others more like Christ. Sometimes Indonesians can see our posture in these situations better than we can see it ourselves.

Of course, there's a place to bring a word of counsel or even rebuke to a church. Paul certainly modeled this in his epistles to the Corinthians and Philippians. And just as we Westerners should be willing to humble ourselves to the perspectives of our Indonesian brothers and sisters (so long as they don't violate clear biblical principles or rules), they should be willing to reciprocate should we have a word of biblical wisdom or admonition to offer. We're not just disinterested observers or cultural relativists. We all have a role to play in keeping our churches on track. That's the "body life" prescribed by the New Testament, wherein hands need feet, eyes need ears, and so on. And in neither the West nor the East is church discipline an optional elective should a congregation need to draw scriptural lines. But in all congregations, whatever criticism or judgment might be needed should be graciously deliberate, not triumphant or petulant, not petty or hair-triggered. Otherwise, who could stand? No, we are to bear with one another in love and respect, long-suffering instead of snippy or easily disdainful.

Moving to Indonesia, we arrived at a place where there was no Baptist church, but we didn't want to isolate ourselves on Sunday morning, sticking strictly to worship at home within our family. We thought it important to be a part of a local church whose convictions and practice were as close to ours as possible. Indeed, we found a body of believers in a remote area who were not even aware of our relatively minor denominational differences, nor would they likely have cared. Furthermore, they may well have been amenable to counsel from our home church should puzzles have arisen.

I think it is also important to note that a church is not made up of members who are all "mouths" or "hands," because that is not a "body." That is more like a manmade organization, which could also be a very positive parachurch organization, like Cru and Pioneers. Those are important organizations, but are not local churches. And those of us who live in Indonesia are really not active parts of congregations in the US either, because they do not see us and live near us; they cannot hold us accountable and guide us as would a local body of believers, no matter how much we communicate with them. They are too far away. They can definitely have a voice in our lives, but they are not the local church for those living overseas. The concept of the authority of an autonomous, geographically local body of believers in our lives is very baptistic. Thus, we should be very careful in giving reasons why being faithful to, and submitting to, a geographically local church does not apply to us.

If we do find a promising church to be a part of, one very practical way to see our commitment level to our local congregation is in how much of our personal finances we are willing to put towards it. I have heard pastors in the US say that if you want to see the commitment level of a person to a certain church, look at their checkbooks. And as seen in the parable of the widow's mite, this is not just a dollar amount, but more about an appropriate level of financial sacrifice. And the Lord cares about the way that we give. If we don't give to our local church body in a way that is more about being seen by God than by men, and if we don't give sacrificially in proportion to the amount of money we receive, those are problems. Fellow Indonesian church members typically feel as though they are under the authority of the church and that they should make the church a priority. We should feel the same way if we live in Indonesia as believers, because this is being faithful to what the Lord has called all believers to do.

Indonesians can see that we have a high salary because of the houses we live in, the things that we buy, how often we travel, and because we are from America. I am not talking about company budgets and other people's money that we may have been entrusted with. I am talking about our personal money. Indonesians usually cannot delineate between the two, and that's really not important. The important thing is that we are faithful financially to the local Body of Christ the Lord has called us to be a part of and submit to at some level. If an Indonesian in our church asks us to contribute to something that is a priority for that church, is that really a sign that they just care about money? Could it also be that Indonesian knows that we do not contribute ten percent of our income to our local church, and they are trying to help us be faithful? If the actual thing the money is going towards is not a personal priority of ours, is that a reason just to give a very small percentage of our salary? Would we be that picky with how a church spends our tithe in the US? It would be tough for me to justify not giving ten percent of our income towards the local body of believers that we are a part of. Because of cultural and other issues, we may not choose to give all of it to the finance committee or elders of the church to decide what they want to do with it. This is not because they are spiritually inferior, but it has to do with vast differences in economics and cultures. Rich people in the US who go to churches in rural areas or to churches with smaller budgets need to exercise the same caution. But though these economic and cultural issues are hard to navigate, I would feel unfaithful if we did not contribute ten percent of our income to the work of local ministry, and I would try to do more than that if we had the means to do so. I think it is a part of recognizing the authority of our local church, what they deem important, and being a member in good standing with that church.

There are a couple of examples in the book of Acts that undergird the financial responsibility I feel towards the local church. In Acts chapter 5, we read that Ananias and Sapphira died because they lied to the Holy Spirit about money. They were not required to sell their land and give it to the church, even though many (maybe even the majority) in that congregation were doing so. Their sin was that they did not give the percentage of their land sale that they said they were giving. Are we living in a way such that we say (with our actions) to our fellow Indonesian church members (and the Holy Spirit) that we are giving ten percent of our income to the betterment of the local church of which we're a part when in reality we are not? Are we in effect lying to ourselves and the Holy Spirit about the percentage of our income we're giving to our local church and about how faithful we're being with our personal finances? We each need to answer that for ourselves, but as the pastor in America said, he can probably take a look at our check books and find out the real answer.

Then we could look to Paul and the Jerusalem offering, a fairly significant event in the book of Acts, and something Paul also talks about in other letters (1 Cor 16:1-4; 2 Cor 8:1-9:15; Rom 15:14-32). This offering that he raised among Gentiles for the Jerusalem church was so important to him that he was willing to face hostility (Rom 15:30-31) and was even arrested in Jerusalem in part because of it (Acts 24:17). Here we see Gentiles giving to a church far away from them because of a need that they saw in Judea, not because Jerusalem required it of them, and not because they didn't have their own needs in Ephesus, Antioch, and the surrounding area. The Gentile churches were not frozen with indecision because of how worthy they thought the church in Jerusalem was. Rather, they saw the economic situation in Jerusalem and took the initiative to help the church in Jerusalem with a significant offering as a show of their support and solidarity. This financial gift was a tangible expression of the generous heart of Gentile believers. They showed they could see the need of the Jerusalem church and demonstrated their willingness to contribute without the Jerusalem church's specifying where they needed the money. I see Western churches and akin to the Gentile believers Paul represented. I want to go above and beyond what is asked of me because I know the situation in Indonesia, and I would want all of my Indonesian brothers and sisters to have no doubt that I am willing to sacrifice financially for them and that is a priority to me. I know it is hard to know how to do this well, but in spite of this difficulty, I would say our default position should be to give above and beyond ten percent rather than to not give at all, because that shows where our heart is and how well we know what our local Indonesian church needs.

All of these things contribute towards my conviction that we should be contributing at least ten percent of our income locally for the good of our local church. The part each person needs to contribute and where is an individual decision. But we should be careful not to, in effect, "lie" to ourselves, others, and the Holy Spirit that we are sacrificially giving this ten percent locally to support our local church.

If we are truly being faithful to the local church with our finances, we should not determine alone how this money should be used. It should not be directed only towards just what we think is important, even though we do have a voice since we are a part of this body. Sometimes, though, we can contribute directly towards things we know are important to the church without putting the cash in their hands since we know their situation. But we should also give a portion of our funds to be spent as the local church decides, while being generous toward needs that may arise among local believers whom we know and trust, especially those called there for ministry. We are called to be good local church members, and if we do not give, it may be that we are standing in judgment on the church, as someone above that church, and that is not our position. If we find a good church, we should support it, and not let the bad experiences of others, and other churches we have been a part of, keep us from doing the good we should do.

It's important to make sure we are not setting ourselves up to be judged as unfaithful with what he has entrusted us: "Everyone to whom much was given, of him much will be required, and from him to whom they entrusted much, they will demand the more" (Lk 12:48), and "as we have opportunity, let us do good to everyone, and especially to those who are of the household of faith" (Gal 6:10). Let's not be the unfaithful person who buries his "talent," and is afraid to take risks, because the Lord might take away what He has entrusted to us and give it to someone else who has been faithful to take risks and multiply what he has been given. "For to everyone who has will more be given, and he will have an abundance. But from the one who has not, even what he has will be taken away" (Mt 25:29). Someone else who has been more faithful and taken more risk with what the Lord has given them could even be an Indonesian believer we look down upon. God might give our "talent" to them and take it away from us. God sees what is happening in our lives and in our churches so much clearer than we do, and we should never think that we as Westerners are above approach where we live in Indonesia and with the believers around us.

CHAPTER 7

The Second Community: Near-Culture "Outsiders"

When Westerners decide to spend several years overseas, is this time more akin to visiting the wild nature of a National Park where visitors are to "leave no trace," or the more industrious charge of the Boy Scouts to "try to leave this world a little better than you found it?" The US National Park Service has seven principles for how to "Leave No Trace," hoping that when we're gone, it will look as if no one had been there so that those who follow can enjoy nature as God created it. People usually don't visit National Parks to see what improvements mankind has made to nature, but to see something that has a natural cycle and a life of its own, a situation that mankind can degrade. There are parts of the natural world that we will never tame and that are far beyond our reach and understanding. It takes some humility to realize that nature is often better off without us, but mankind has not been placed on this earth to serve the needs of nature. As image bearers of God, we've been created to harness nature for our purposes and to tame its wildness, albeit in a limited way in limited places. We need to understand what we can change, what we can influence, and what is out of our hands. We aim to work in concert with the laws of nature, in order to leave nature "better than we found it" in those places where we try to alter it.

The founder of the Boy Scouts, Sir Robert Baden-Powell, told scouts to "try to leave this world a little better than you found it" in his last message. After an inspiring meeting with Baden-Powell, Juliette Gordan Lowe established the Girl Scouts that same year.[52] Those of us who have known Eagle Scouts and are familiar with the program, know that it develops leaders and has a well-earned reputation for producing individuals who know how to make a positive difference in the world. While "leaving no trace" and "leaving a place better than you found" seem to be contradictory, the Boy Scouts subscribe to both. As with most things, we need a sense of balance, and I would argue that living overseas as a Westerner calls for balancing these two seemingly contradictory mindsets.

When it comes to interacting with others, especially in financial matters, there is a sense of satisfaction in accomplishing a certain task and "leaving no trace." I had a job for several summers in college for which I would drive a box truck to different universities throughout the United States with one other individual. Working with a campus organization, we'd man a poster sale booth and give a percentage of the profits to our host group. Each time we shut the back of the truck, shook hands with our campus contact, and headed off to the next campus, there was a sense of freedom and closure with previous sales. It was a mutually beneficial relationship, but one that was very limited in positive impact on the school. We sellers essentially "left no trace" as we earned money for college and for the company. But as someone who moved his family overseas for several years, my greatest apprehension was that when I eventually returned to America was that I would "leave no trace"—that my time in Indonesia would be like a footprint in the sand along the beach: After a few waves wash up on the shore, it would be as if I were never there.

Those who have owned a house understand equity—the difference between reducing the principle with a mortgage payment and paying rent to someone else who owns a house. Those who prefer to "leave no trace" overseas surely want to build up some "relational equity" and "spiritual equity" with the people and churches with which they're involved overseas, but I would consider that a given with anyone who moves overseas for reasons related to the social good. And, of course, changed hearts are eternal gains. But I'm going on to argue that we should also "leave a place better than we found it" when it comes to actual *financial* equity for those with whom we work. It's not either-or affair, but rather a matter of balance. As Westerners living overseas, we bring quite an array of financial resources, and it would be odd if we limited our concern to only relational and spiritual impact. Of course, there is need for caution. We wouldn't want to leave a trail of waste and destruction that poisoned an area and made it a little worse than we found it. Indeed, unhealthy dependency, shattered relationships, and unrealized expectations are all real challenges for those who work cross-culturally on financial endeavors, but there are ways to avoid these outcomes. Even if they do tend to rear their ugly heads time to time, it does not mean that investing in others financially is not worth the effort. None of the meaningful things we do in our lives are perfect and without their problems. As several have encouraged us, we should "do hard things."[53]

Around 2009, I met two Indonesian men who became my colleagues. They both came from other islands where they'd experienced their share of hardship, and they'd found their way to the island of Buton. One had just been married in South Sulawesi, and the other soon married on Buton. One was from the island of Timor, the eastern side of which made headlines in the late 1990s when it separated from the nation of Indonesia, and the United Nations had to get involved. This man was from the western side of Timor, up in the mountains, specifically from an area where a Christian revival occurred in the 1960s and '70s. (It's recounted in the book, *Like a Mighty Wind*, by Mel Tari.)[54] When he was in high school, the youth minister at his church led this man into a deeper relationship with Christ, to the point where he and others decided to go to Discipleship Training School (DTS) with Youth With A Mission (YWAM), located in the majority Christian Toraja area of South Sulawesi. During this time with YWAM, he grew in faith and knowledge of how to walk with the Lord, and, at one point, he spent a few months on Buton serving with a local church to get some practical ministry experience. During this time, the Lord planted a seed in his heart for the people of Buton, and, years later, he moved there, not knowing exactly what he would do for work. He was just convinced that was where he was supposed to live.

His wife had a story all her own. Her parents passed away when she was young, so she moved in with some of her close relatives in a nearby city in Western Sulawesi. These years were hard, as her role with this family was similar to that of Cinderella. She eventually decided to run away and live with another part of her extended family on Java. So, as a teenager, she rode a bus for about twelve hours to Makassar, then stowed away on a boat for a couple of days to reach Java. Miraculously, she was able to connect with her aunt, and she spent several years with them before ending up at DTS with YWAM. Her time of ministry was spent serving at an orphanage on the majority-Hindu island of Bali. She and the man from Timor started to have feelings for each other at DTS, but they decided they should both minister for at least a year in other areas to see if the Lord would eventually bring them back together. It turned out that this lady had an aunt who lived with her husband on Buton, so she moved there around the same time this young man did, and they felt the Lord wanted them together. So after about a year engagement, they were married and started to raise a family on Buton.

The other man came from the island of Borneo, and was from the Dayak people, who are famous for tattooing all of their bodies and living in longhouses in the jungle. He came from a Muslim family, but when he was young, both of his parents passed away. While the extended family was trying to figure out what to do with him and his other siblings, a man came from Toraja and offered free schooling to any child in their village who was willing to attend a Christian boarding school in West Sulawesi.

This young man and one of his cousins agreed, so they left their village and spent the next ten years or so at this school along with a couple of hundred other students. It was a meaningful time in his life, and the school also helped him get started with a college program on Java. He didn't complete college, but started working for a wealthy individual making deliveries and doing odd jobs throughout the large city of Surabaya. This allowed him to get on his feet financially, before he decided to enter the ministry and pastor a small church. He then felt called to return to Sulawesi for ministry, and he entered a training program that would help him learn some skills to start a business. While in Makassar at this training, he met his wife, who was working in the area and was from Toraja. They went to the same church, and decided to get married before they would move to the island where they felt they were supposed to live and work, Buton. These two families were living in the same city as I was, and our paths crossed just before I considered starting a tourism company in 2010.

In the late 1990s, of all the provinces in Indonesia, Southeast Sulawesi had the fewest foreign visitors. While this place was very beautiful, it was not really on the way to anywhere, unless you were travelling by ship. Most foreigners travel by air in this day and age, so the cards were stacked against anyone trying to start a tourism business there. But the first mayor of the city where we lived saw the tourism potential of the province despite transportation challenges, and I was intrigued. So, after several years of working with the Indonesian Department of Education through an NGO providing English native speakers to the province, I made a shift to tourism and started a branch of an adventure tourism business that sought to bring Westerners to the province for activities such as scuba diving, eco-tours, and cultural visits to remote islands and villages. The people were very hospitable throughout the province and loved to have foreign guests visit and stay with them. But, in general, they were also very content to keep living their lives as they had for generations, and it was hard for me to meet anyone locally who was able to see the adventure in going out to visit other villages in the province. As with most of us, familiarity breeds indifference, so my first tour guides were the two Indonesians mentioned above, who had moved to this city just like me (between 2007 and 2010). But since they were from other parts of the country with different cultures, Buton offered fresh experiences.

As our first guests started to trickle in, we started to work on building an office and also living space for one of our guides. We soon discovered that the people of Buton considered buying land and building a house as one of the most important steps in becoming Butonese. Those who were committed enough to invest money in physical assets were clearly "one of them," and most Butonese considered acquiring your own house as a rite of manhood. If you had a place to live, you could sustain yourself and raise a family. With the Butonese living so far off the beaten path in Indonesia, they were used to being able to sustain themselves with little help from the outside, as long as they had a place to live. Living on remote islands has made the Butonese very resilient and self-reliant. So, over time we realized that the long-term health of the business required that we invest in property, for us to weather hard times when we had few guests and also for our guides and us to be considered local and committed to the area.

We also learned that being married with children who were being raised on Buton was important for our guides' longevity. There will always be a role for singles in our tourism business, and some of the singles we invest in locally could eventually marry and raise families on Buton, but most of them have moved eventually to other parts of the country—for work, to marry, or because their extended family provided more opportunities elsewhere. Those tour guides who decided to commit to raising their families on Buton, not only gave our business the stability and reputation it needed, but it also provided for individuals who needed a place to live and were invested enough to contribute to, and manage, properties which could serve as their houses and places of business. Almost everyone on Buton is bi-vocational, and in this job market, finding a suitable house and paying rent are major hurdles for those who wish to move to the island. We soon found out that if an Indonesian has a stable place to live, his extended family members won't call them to come back to their province of origin, but will ask if their children might come live with our tour guides.

These early lessons on the importance of properties for the long-term health of our business on Buton gave rise to most of the lessons in this book. It is not a natural thing to decide to invest money in a remote part of Indonesia if the Return on Investment (ROI) is not clear. It is hard to sell properties on Buton, because most people do not have a large amount of money to pay out at one time and loans are very difficult to come by. Consequently, they build little by little and "rough it" in partially finished houses for most of their lives. Those who have the backing to build a house usually make the most profit personally off the way they manage construction, especially if they are doing it on behalf of a company or a government project. So, the best scenario is that you own property built for your purposes, that you have someone committed to the property and its upkeep, and that it has long-term, multipurpose flexibility. This requires a long-term commitment and the ability to stick it out in remote places as a foreigner—not always a situation we can control, especially when it comes to immigration issues. But even immigration authorities, with the increasing popularity and access of investment visas, look favorably on those who are willing to invest financially in an area. They're seen as worth keeping around. The businesses and individuals you interact with during these financial endeavors can also develop into long-time friends, just as they would in your home country.

Of course, in a cross-cultural environment we all have a lot more to learn. The way we were raised to think, is probably not the way those around us were raised to think. And most of these cross-cultural lessons cannot be learned in books, but are learned through experience. Still, a book is not a bad place to start.

After developing a clear long-term vision of what we want to accomplish to "make a place better than we left it," balanced with "leaving no trace," we must continually do the work in our own hearts to ensure we are not primarily trying to justify ourselves or our presence in an area by what we accomplish. Rather, our focus is on others, whom we're trying to shape positively. These will ideally be mutually beneficial relationships, but we need to be able to identify the moments where sacrifice is required on our part, or where we need to take calculated risks for someone else. I hope this book will provide both the theoretical and practical tools needed to help cross-cultural workers move in the right direction in their endeavors overseas, with a balance of both theoretical and practical goals.

CHAPTER 8

Appropriate Financial Responsibility

F or a story related to the importance of managing well the things that we are entrusted with, we can look at the parable of the talents (Mt 25:14-30). The amount of money we make or the value of assets that we are responsible for connects, positively or negatively, with our dependence on God. Providing money and assets to individuals whose hearts are not in the right place to receive them is unwise, just as it is unwise to provide money and assets to individuals in such amounts that it tempts them beyond what they are able to bear and contributes to their falling into sin, even if their hearts were in the right place to begin with. Each person has to be evaluated individually in these two areas, and any support provided to them needs to be appropriate and viewed as such by those around them.

It is usually wise to know someone personally and see the way that they work before they are provided money for a service. This is not always possible, so in dealing with unfamiliar personnel, a contract or document should be in place to assure that support is limited in time and/or scope. If we see that an Indonesian can live on what he has, even if it is a small amount, without complaining or always bringing up the topic when they are around us, this suggests they can be content with what the Lord is providing. Of course, anyone can sacrifice and rough it for a limited period of time if they are motivated to do so, but when it comes to long-term support, we need to be sure we are actually providing enough for our employees to live on. No matter how much someone depends on the Lord, if their family or they are not personally making enough to provide for their basic subsistence, especially when they are spending their money wisely, short-term survival is not a fair indicator. I would want them to tell me if they felt they just couldn't manage on what they were receiving. And most of the time when I provide a salary, I have already seen what others I have known longer can survive on (and thrive on). So, I observe new individuals to see how they manage their money, and at what point they think it is important to let me know about financial issues they may be having. If I feel as though an employee manages his money wisely, can be content with a small salary, and can still be effective in his work, then I believe I've found the type of person I want to bless with more. Most Western companies and organizations make sure employees aren't just scraping by, but also have enough to send kids to college, buy imported food, and even maintain a house in the West if they use their money wisely. We Westerners shouldn't suppose that our good income is compatible with a vital relationship with God, while at the same time thinking that Indonesians can only grow spiritually if they are kept down at the survival level.

The other common challenge when it comes to finances and Indonesians is deciding whether putting an asset or amount of money into their hands is more than they are able to handle without stumbling. It doesn't concern ethnicity but rather assessing their economic standard and determining what they're accustomed to handling. Most Indonesians whom I know and trust do not want to be responsible for an asset or amount of money whose loss would lead to their financial ruin or a violation of trust they could never repair.

In the West, we typically have insurance to cover such issues, but Indonesians don't usually have that kind of protection. It is possible that putting too much financial responsibility on them will pave the way for Satan to approach them with compromising notions. To lessen temptation, it's best to not put large amounts of cash (such as several years' annual salary) into an Indonesian's hand, lest they abscond with it. This can be especially risky if we are not on site at the time, or the money transaction is something that only the two of us know about. These circumstances make it easier for someone to have a lapse in judgment and keep the money, especially if they are not committed long-term to the area where they are living and are detached enough that they could leave on a moment's notice and never come back if the right opportunity came long—not that your friends would usually do this; just that you don't want to put them in that position.

Another set of problems concerns the kind of assets that we entrust to Indonesians. Because of the way some NGOs operate overseas, most of us have a car in our name that we bought at the dealership, and by all legal aspects we own it. The NGO probably doesn't have many personnel sell their car and run off with the money, because most of us have owned cars in the past and could buy a car in the US if we needed to; it's an asset we're used to handling. Even though the NGO basically gave us a car, we know that we have really just been entrusted with using this car, and, if we sold it, we would return the proceeds to the NGO. But this is an informal agreement between us and the NGO, and if we wanted to get away with selling it and keeping the money, we could probably make it happen without anyone's stopping us. But since we need a car to do our job and the NGO pays us a monthly salary, we aren't very tempted to sell it because we would lose our transportation, our salary would be cut off, and we would probably need to buy our own ticket home at a cost greater than our return on the sale.

You can bet that the NGO's lawyers and financial personnel have thought through all those risks and know it really wouldn't be worth it to us. We need to put ourselves in the same shoes as the NGO administrators when we entrust Indonesians with assets, being sure it makes more sense for them to keep the asset in line with the purpose for which it was entrusted. We do, indeed, have Indonesian employees in Sulawesi who've been entrusted with assets that, for all intents and purposes, they may technically own, but they know that these assets are not theirs and that they've been entrusted to them to use in line with their work. The same goes for the cars we ourselves get from an NGO.

And then there's the matter of houses. In each situation, I've explored the network of relationships that are connected to the building, have put a variety of legal documents in place, and held on to the original deeds. I know how complicated it is to sell a house and how much the Indonesian needs a place to live. And, of course, I can stop their salary if I need to. So, it's probably not worth it for them to try to sell their house because of the damage it would do to their lives, and because it would have a low likelihood of success. This is all in addition to the fact that I trust them, which I hope would be enough to deter them. But again, I also know that if there is a way that they think they could really get away with selling the house and running away with the cash, Satan could use that to destroy a believer who was wholly dependent on God before that burden was put on them. I would never want to be a potential tool of Satan in that way, so I try to be as careful as possible while also trying to bless others with the same measure that I have been blessed. For to "everyone to whom much was given, of him much will be required" (Luke 12:48).

There are many specific situations where we know of colleagues working for NGOs and other Indonesians who have succumbed to temptations to be untrustworthy with their finances. All of us are susceptible to those temptations, and the NGO chose us as field personnel because, using a variety of evaluative tools, they decided we were depending on God and trustworthy. We need to do the same careful evaluation of our employees and of other people we work with. Once we have judged them honorable, then we should feel free to bless them even as NGO's have blessed us in so many ways. We shouldn't be so afraid of making a mistake with money that our fellow coworkers suffer and barely make a living when it is easily within our power to help them out. They should be able to save money for their children's future and inheritance, as well as have funds to go on vacation, buy land, and buy a motorcycle. Whether they have these things or not is not a measure of whether they depend on God or not. But we all know that money applied in the wrong situation in the wrong way can negatively affect people, so we should exercise wisdom, with the counsel of others, before extending trust.

One must also consider whether (and to what extent) it is wise to discuss financial arrangements and transactions with others, including local employees. This concerns the amount they receive from us and the assets with which they are entrusted. Our account should make sense and sound fair, and, if someone asks us about something financial and we are tempted to lie about it, that should be a big red flag to us. But we should still use discretion, and the details of these things should usually just be limited to discussions with others in whom we have confidence. Naturally, some of the more visible blessings will be apparent to acquaintances and even the general public. These things should all line up with who we are, and who our employees are, so they don't create situations that could negatively impact our business and work. We should be comfortable explaining all of these things in a way that makes sense to everyone. This can mean a difficult balancing act at times, but it is definitely worth it since there are few others in a position like ours to use the financial resources at our disposal in a way that blesses our Indonesian friends and employees, while managing the accountability of these resources as well.

CHAPTER 9

Giving and Earning

In the book *Poverty of Nations*, the authors ask "What kind of economic system best motivates and enables people to create more goods and services of value?" They argue that the role of the government and the leaders of a country should be more than working for more production, but also seeking to provide the "right conditions for innovation and entrepreneurship to happen in a free-market system."[55] Remote places of Indonesia need people to create things of value that other people are willing to pay for. It's not the same as donating money or sending aid to a place because we want to help them. It's about creating a service or product that people are willing to purchase, whether or not they care about other people; it's about business. In *The Tragedy of American Compassion*, Marvin Olasky explains that if all the money paid to programs fighting poverty by the US government were distributed evenly among the poor, they would have enough money to not be categorized as people living in "poverty." [56] But the problem is not about the total money given; it's about how people earn and use that money. Being poor is just a symptom of a larger problem, usually related to how people make and spend their money and the opportunities they have available to them. Just throwing money at the problem will not solve it. Those funds will always disappear, and more will be needed—a problem we see repeated over and over again in welfare systems.

When a business is created, it usually requires a larger amount of money at the start, with the hope that this initial capital will not only provide an ongoing means of financial support monthly for everyone involved, but that there will also eventually be enough extra money earned to pay back the initial capital investment and make even more profit in the future. For those who take out loans to start a business, making back that initial capital investment is crucial, because they need to pay back the loan. If they don't need to pay back the initial investment, then their main concern is to generate enough income each month so they can live, which requires their using the assets and training they acquired and developed with that initial capital investment wisely. The business's making long term profit is just icing on the cake—something that not all businesses are able to do well, which is fine. The basic requirement is to meet the ongoing needs of those involved by providing a service or product of value that people will purchase. This is best described as "earning money" or "earning a living," which is different from being "given" money.

When money is "given" or "donated" to someone, that means that the person who receives the gift is not creating a marketable thing of value. People give money to causes, expecting nothing in return (except maybe a tax break and good feelings about themselves). They know that not everyone is in a position to "earn" enough money to make a living, because of where they live, their education and training level, or some other factor that may be out of their control. This does not mean that the people "given" money are not working; it just means that they are not doing something that generates money sufficient for their needs, even though their work may be praiseworthy. The bottom line is that the people giving the money are free to give to the cause or not; the amount they give is arbitrary, depending on their wishes; and someone else receives the tangible benefit of this money.

The person who receives this "given" or "donated" money may be doing physical work or not. There are people who work for non-profits (NGOs, etc.) who are entrusted with getting this money to the right place in a legal way, which takes work. These NGO workers are earning money from the legal entity that hired them, because they are doing something that creates the opportunity for the NGO to keep receiving donations. This level of work is somewhat gray, because they are "earning" money by doing work, but this work isn't creating a product or service that is being bought. So these NGO workers are not earning money in the same way that a business earns it; the money for their employment is "given" not "earned," even if they are personally "earning" their salary.

Then, the next level down are the people who are "given" money without doing anything to earn it. This is often the "cause" or "goal" of an NGO, like giving money or food to poor people, usually to help with a temporary situation like a disaster. But then there is money given in the form of assets or capital to get a business going, which they use to "earn" money long term. These grants are usually one-time affairs or keyed to a limited period of time. But the recipient is eventually expected to "earn" money like everyone else. They may always feel a certain level of gratefulness for help they were "given" to start a business or get by after a particularly difficult time, but they will always need to get to a point where they "earn" money. When they start to "earn" money through creating a service or product of value that people are willing to pay for, then they are no longer in this category of people "given" something; they're now earners.

The only people who are in an ongoing state of being sustained by "given" money are those who administer the work of NGOs, even though they may be working very hard. They live and work in the gray area of whether they are actually "earning" money or living on money that is "given" to them. This does not mean that the role of people at this level is not as important as that of those who "earn" money; it just means that if donors no longer feel compelled to support their cause, then they have to stop doing what they are doing, or do it without getting paid. They rely on people who feel as though what they are doing is important. Unfortunately, it's possible that NGO workers without accountability do nothing of value and still receive money because contributors assume they are doing a good job. We see this less-than-ideal situation all the time in the world. Consequently, the key is accountability, with ways to measure effectiveness in contributing towards the causes people support. In contrast, people who have jobs that "earn" money usually do not have the luxury of receiving money when they are not working effectively, because the moment they stop providing a valuable product or service, then people stop paying for it.

On the Aroma Islands, our closest Indonesian partners who are shareholders in businesses were all "given" money in the past in the form of capital to get their businesses going. All of them who are still receiving a salary are now "earning" a salary by creating a product or service that people are willing to pay for. They no longer rely on donations. So, they've not been "given" money for several years. The only people on our team who receive "given" money are the Westerners who have financial support from their home country. Our Indonesian employees and business owners are all "earning" their money in conjunction with the businesses they operate or the properties they own.

CHAPTER 10

The Role of Westerners

Westerners living in Indonesia must learn to navigate issues and criticisms that can arise in the minds of Indonesians because of differences in the culture and economy of their home countries. It is easy for Westerners to have a hard time understanding this Indonesian viewpoint because we are so wrapped up in our own culture and have a hard time looking at the situation objectively. It has taken me many years, but with the help of several Indonesians (some friends, some not), I think I understand. To focus this discussion, I will refer to two critiques by a Christian Indonesian man who had previous work experience for several years in Singapore, and moved to our province to manage and train a team to start a boat building business. In general, I don't think his heart was in the right place to make these judgments and comments, but I do understand what he was saying, and there is some truth to it.

The first comment he made was in a group setting of about eighty cross-cultural workers, where about ninety-five percent were Indonesians, and five percent were American. It was his view that Westerners were not really needed for cross-cultural work in our province, because they required a large amount of funding and, most of the time, they just reported success stories about Indonesians with whom they partnered. He thought that the money invested in Westerners living overseas wasn't really worth the service they provided as middlemen in the reporting process. So, this leads me to ask what unique things do we as Westerners involved in starting cross-cultural business ventures bring to the table, and is it worth the expense of getting us here and sustaining our work? In long-term business operations, we play second to near-culture cross-cultural workers. We'll be less eloquent, not really fit in, and miss important cultural cues. We social entrepreneurs often want to help small communities, and being able to interact with them effectively is one of the most essential aspects of our work. So, if Indonesians are better at this, why would we ever pay an American worker $3,000 a month over supporting an Indonesian with $300 a month? Or to put it another way, why would we choose to support one Western entrepreneur family over ten Indonesian families? It would probably come to more like one American to fifteen Indonesians when you factor in rental, visas, and transportation to and from America. I think the hard fact of this financial imbalance should never be taken for granted by Western cross-cultural workers and entrepreneurs.

Before I continue this discussion, I want to make it clear that I think it is good that Westerners are deciding to move to Indonesia (and other countries in Southeast Asia) to pursue endeavors as social entrepreneurs. At the same time, I have no problem with having hard discussions about the concrete facts regarding the finances required to support Americans overseas, even at the risk of getting my feelings hurt. If we as Americans take for granted the amount of money it takes to keep us overseas in relation to our Indonesian brothers and sisters, we can become discontented with the relatively low salary we receive compared to those in the West. We might spend our time thinking about the restaurants in the West that we don't get to visit, the kids' sports programs and educational opportunities not available in our region, and the difficulties with living in such a "foreign" culture. This constant remembrance of our home culture and the sacrifices we have made is totally normal for those newly arrived overseas, but there should be a point where we are able to see more clearly how much we have been blessed to be able to live where few other Westerners live, how we are supported very generously considering the cost of living where we live, and that we have a great deal of freedom in our work. Our perspective on the situation should mature over time to a point where we realize how much more we make than our Indonesian brothers and sisters. Any judgment we make about the way that Indonesians manage their finances and depend on the Lord financially are probably taken with a grain of salt by the Indonesians we engage. We could consider how we might feel if Bill Gates or Jeff Bezos were friends who kept criticizing us over how we used our relatively low salaries, suggesting we were low on wisdom and generosity. Meanwhile, they're flying all over the country in private jets, eating the best food, and acting put upon if we ask them for financial help in some way. If we Westerners are not generous and creative in how we use our finances in Indonesia, most of our Indonesian brothers and sisters will probably see that as a lack of self-awareness on our part, a failure to appreciate how much we have been blessed financially and how we could possibly use that good fortune to benefit others in need. I think God sees this as a heart issue as well.

We should also be self-aware about our spiritual role in Indonesia. If we think that Indonesian believers should always listen to and value what we have to say about the will of God for their lives, we probably think more highly of ourselves than we should. We are at a particular disadvantage in this area, because "it is easier for a camel to go through the eye of a needle than for a rich person to enter the kingdom of God" (Mt 19:24). We must be good stewards of the funds with which we have been entrusted with and give generously, just as we have been blessed generously. I can think of three primary ways that we can be social entrepreneurs worthy of being financed by others.

We can play a role in bringing together Indonesians of different backgrounds and organizations cross-culturally because of our status as

Westerners, because we can overcome petty differences and arguments that would impede cooperation among Indonesian workers. Westerners are not above these things, because in our own teams of Westerners and organizations in our home countries, internal issues always arise, and we have trouble working together within our own culture. But as outsiders, we can break through many of these obstacles for our Indonesian partners because we can stand outside a number of their cultural pressures, offering different perspectives, and our financial independence can help to some extent. In our role as mediator among Indonesians of various backgrounds and priorities, I don't think the real problem is how much or how little we are involved, but how effectively we can work together with those of other cultures being truly inter-dependent, or mutually dependent on one another. There is much to say about the positive aspects of independence and autonomy, of which we are proud of in America, but in cross-cultural work overseas, it can be a liability. Our Indonesian friends with whom we have chosen to partner closely need to know that we are going to be fair to everyone, that we understand their unique situations, and that we are willing to sacrifice things for their well-being. This role of the Westerner in bringing people together seems most effective with at least one Westerner on the ground (locally and long-term, ideally with their family) who is skilled in this area.

Westerners also usually have extensive networks throughout the region and the world, connections we can bring to bear to provide training and different viewpoints. Western educational institutions usually have a more rigorous educational system than what you find in most Indonesian schools, especially those in remote areas. We need to make sure we are drawing Indonesian friends and partners together to understand concepts that enrich, contextualize, and even transcend notions at play in the venture.

In order for our presence to be worthwhile, we should constantly be interpreting things that are happening locally, by using insights gained through higher education. This role as interpreter serves both Indonesian partners and American supporters or those pursuing similar business ventures in other parts of the country or region. I would argue that our ability to see and explain from a Western mindset what is happening locally in Indonesia is another one of our essential tasks. This will not only build understanding and trust among those we work with locally and in Southeast Asia; it encourages financial support from more affluent venture capitalists in the West, resources to be applied more effectively in poorer parts of the world.

We are probably all familiar with the argument that the millions of dollars spent by Americans each year to patronize overseas tourism could just be sent to Indonesians who own other small businesses, and this could fund everything they ever wanted. But would these funds go to the right place, and might that much money going to Indonesian partners corrupt most of them because of the great temptations associated with financial dealings? Many American workers in Indonesia are also unclear over how to use financial resources effectively. (This is a primary reason I decided to write this book.) Westerners must be able to make wise decisions about which individuals to work with and to what extent. They'll need to keep a healthy balance in these relationships with individuals and employees who'll be making judgments about whether they are being treated fairly compared to others. This balance, and the span of close supervision it involves, needs to make sense to other Indonesians in our circle of influence. Indeed, a large amount of our success in bringing Indonesians from different backgrounds together, and leveraging our education and networks for the good of the business, will depend on choosing the right individuals to work with.

To help illustrate the delicate nature of being able to foster trust cross-culturally and how seemingly minor decisions can lead to major unintended consequences, we will hear another critique brought by an Indonesian brother commenting on the role of Westerners overseas. It helps illustrate a financial issue that is the outworking of the different mindsets. This Indonesian man felt God leading him to move his family out of Singapore to a relatively small city in Eastern Indonesia to lead a boat manufacturing business in partnership with an American, and they started with about six unmarried male trainees who moved with them to learn the trade during an initial year of training. This married Indonesian manager saw himself as the one driving operations, and he would teach most of the classes for these six guys, as well as live together with them and his family. Within this context, he led the day-to-day operations of the training center and was the primary teacher. Initially, the Westerner taught the manager and the others how to make molds and fiberglass boats, but soon the Indonesians could do these things on their own.

The American was seen as the main source of income for this endeavor through his connection with more affluent Americans. He also possessed the technical expertise in fiberglass boat building, so he could accommodate custom orders and answer special questions. This American had a large family and a large house with a large yard a mile or so down the road, and he taught some classes, but was not as heavily involved in daily business operations as the Indonesian team leader. Still, he was seen as the leader of the whole operation because he was the link that funded everything, and he had business experience with boat building that they hoped would help support everyone financially in the future. I believe both of these men and their families had good intentions in pursuing this social and business venture, and, after what happened, I can understand both of their viewpoints. This isn't to say who was right or wrong; it's just to explain what happened and what differences in mindsets and an inability to see another person's point of view can do.

It was very stressful for the American family to live in a relatively remote province of Indonesia with few other Westerners for society. Add to that the stress of homeschooling six children and the pressures of keeping things running financially for a team from another culture. Some American friends in the US knew about these burdens and said they wanted to pay for this American family to take a vacation to Jakarta for several days so they could get refreshed. The family appreciated this gesture and went to Jakarta for about a week to eat at some nice restaurants, go to some nice malls, and maybe fellowship with other Westerners. I would estimate that the roundtrip flights for eight people was about $2,400 ($300 each), and at least two hotel rooms for six nights would be $600 ($100 a night), for a total of $3,000, not counting taxis and other miscellaneous expenses. When they returned from this vacation, they had been living in this remote area for about nine months and they were looking at sending all the single guys, the trainees, out to more remote parts of the province at the one-year mark for survey and marketing purposes. This American was estimating the cost for this, and he could see they were coming up short. So, he asked the team leader to work his Singapore connections for help to underwrite the travels of the six. The Indonesian team leader immediately thought of the American family's recent vacation and was offended, feeling that the Westerner was betraying him and the team.

To understand the mindset of this Indonesian team leader please put aside all your initial thoughts about the distinction between personal and business funds, between budget line items and their purposes. Just think about how an Indonesian could figure that at least $3,000 was spent on vacation for this American family, and probably closer to $4,000 when you consider transportation, entertainment, food, and shopping in Jakarta. If we use an exchange rate of Rp 10,000=$1 (approximately the rate at that time) and guess that the six single guys each received about $100 a month in salary, and the Indonesian team leader received about $300 a month, along with about $100 in miscellaneous monthly water, electricity, and training expenses, this would come to about $1,000 a month to support this Indonesian team. So, this American family just spent 3-4 months of money for their vacation that could have supported the entire Indonesian team, not for vacation, but for buying rice and surviving, as well as working in a remote area.

The Indonesian team leader was used to other Indonesians' (especially government workers administering projects) using money meant for public concerns for their own personal benefit. It involves dishonest dealings and deceitful reporting, typically undermining the quality of the work. No matter what the American says about the reasons for their vacation and where the money came from, the Indonesian team leader sees the American family spending a lot on themselves for a one-week vacation instead of supporting a well-qualified Indonesian team leader and his family and crew for 3-4 months.

We can all identify with the American in this situation, and probably think that he was treated unfairly by the Indonesian who was offended. If we think about it, we should also be able to understand the Indonesian team leader's viewpoint. Not surprising that they view our role and decisions regarding finances as more often based on our own personal comfort and Western cultural expectations instead of concern for how best to conduct business and support our Indonesian employees. Their negative judgment is compounded if they see us spending most of our time at home with our families, pecking away at the computer, and traveling to meetings instead of getting out and engaging with the local communities. They also probably assume we are reporting the business successes of our Indonesian national partners as our own successes. Indonesians can generally see how much money we have coming in and going out, and if we are not directing a significant portion of those funds to support work on the ground, we're asking for major problems. The incident described above led immediately to the dissolution of this team. All the team members scattered to try and find a way to support themselves, with about seventy-five percent of them returning to their home island or country.

CHAPTER 11

From Outer Workings
to Inner Workings

I feel a deep sense of thankfulness every day for the way that friends and family have helped support our social and business endeavors overseas all of these years. This would never have happened without them. The last chapter is not meant to dissuade or discourage those of us who feel called by the Lord to serve overseas; it's just meant to help us think critically about how we can be most effective in our work and what our role in Indonesia actually is. In order to think through these things and still have a peace about pursing social ventures such as these, I have come to understand many spiritual principles which I've outlined in the following chapters, organized into Seven Levels. I hope this can serve as a diagnostic tool to determine where we are spiritually, and what we need to work on, as well as a tool with biblical references and insight to help us grow in the areas where we determine that we are weak.

The most effective application of these principles would begin by taking initiative to understand how others view us, taking extra steps in understanding how others think, and then trying to follow the Lord's leading in how best to serve them. As noted in *The Prophet*, "It is well to give when asked, but it is better to give unasked, through understanding."[57] The most valuable and difficult lessons I have learned overseas deal with financial and property issues with Indonesians. As someone who has run businesses overseas for the past twelve years or so, while trying to set up my employees for success in the future, I have learned how Indonesians can feel like they are being cared for financially. Even to the point where they are comfortable in raising their families outside of their original island, taking financial risks, and inviting other extended family members from their homeland to come live with them and go to school. How to meet these conditions for Indonesians we employ can be especially hard to understand in the West. We appreciate the same things, but the context for receiving them is very different, and silent, less formal understandings among friends are in play. It takes a while to sort out these things.

As we seek to play an important role overseas, worthy of the investment, I'm reminded of a military example. When describing how a logistics unit should support combat units overseas, a Marine friend of mine once said the unit should be careful to avoid becoming a "self-licking ice cream cone." The problem arose when much or virtually all of the equipment and resources they brought overseas was used primarily to support the logistics unit itself, with increasing levels of comfort. The best of the resources never really got to the combat units that they were actually for, and, if the logistics unit just disappeared, things would still look very much the same on the front lines. Westerners living overseas can succumb to the same pitfall. Because of the hardship of adjusting to a different culture, we can become more concerned with our own comfort and forget many of the primary reasons we moved overseas in the first place, to make a positive difference in the lives of those we work with. The Seven Levels material at the end of this book is meant to help all believers diagnose where we might need to do some work on our own hearts, particularly when it comes to justification. When living in a remote area overseas, it is easy to start asking whether you are making a difference, and whether your presence there is justified. The Seven Levels come from my own spiritual journey as a cross-cultural worker, and I hope it will help readers to better understand how believers ideally should all be working together in a selfless way. In Level 1, we must constantly remind ourselves that health, safety, and prosperity should not be our primary goals in life, and when trying to start businesses overseas, we should be more concerned about making enough positive impact in the lives of others to justify our being there in the first place.

Understanding how to apply Level 2 can be very difficult for those of us from the West who move to a "Third World" country. For a number of reasons, most Westerners probably think they will play a very important role in the lives of many Indonesians when they move overseas, because they have more education and more global experiences at their disposal. But in most cases, these advantages just play a supporting role in what will have the most impact—being able to see how people of every race on earth have similar weaknesses and struggles as humans and then having the humility to work alongside those of different nationalities as peers in bringing them together as partners. If we are able to approach our relationships in this way, we will be better equipped to think critically about how we can make a difference in the lives of others. On the other hand, if we are always trying to prove to ourselves (and others) how much more we know or how our ways are better, we will probably miss the wealth of lessons we can learn from people with vastly different backgrounds.

When applying lessons from Level 3, we must be willing to admit when we are wrong, both to God and to others—even to those under our authority, such as our children or our employees. It is very healthy to be able to know when we are wrong (and sometimes even when we aren't wrong) and then act with grace and humility towards those who think we are. We need to be able to suppress defensiveness when we are challenged or questioned. This lesson continues to play itself out in Levels 4, 5, and 6, where we need to learn to look past, or deal patiently with, what we might initially consider a wrong way of doing things by others, especially when these are just differences in opinion or matters of conscience. Most of the time, if we withhold judgment until we've taken the time to really understand the situation, and if we are in a good position to hear what the other person is saying, we can avoid making decisions that we will regret in the long run, and those detrimental to our work.

In applying lessons learned in Level 7, we are better able to expend our energy on the task at hand, instead of upon relationship and leadership issues that plague many businesses. Many leadership challenges in businesses (and other organizations), especially those which are cross-cultural, are actually self-inflicted by the leaders themselves, because they are trying to exert more control than they should and have little margin in their lives to do so well. This does not mean leaders should be laissez-faire in giving direction to people and businesses they lead, but they should try to lead others in a way that would compel them to follow even if they were peers. It is increasingly rare to find a leader who knows the art of leading others with transparency and humility, and in a way that convinces those who follow that he is for them even when it costs him. People want to follow leaders like this. The peace that comes from trusting in the Lord for our justification, and the humility which accompanies this, allows us to better see those we lead for who they are, and see how we can support them in ways that go above and beyond the ways they can support themselves. The following chapters are meant to be tools to help believers grow as disciples of Christ, while also developing a healthy mindset as a cross-cultural leader, starting with the Cross.

CHAPTER 12

The Cross

Those who come to Christ are not just leaving something behind, being saved *from* something when they come to faith; they are also becoming a part of something new. John Stott, in his classic book *The Cross of Christ*, provides four pictures to help us understand what was accomplished by the Cross in order to bring about our salvation.[58] The first picture is of the temple, where a blood sacrifice is required to appease the anger of God—propitiation. This is how God provided a way to avert his own anger. The second picture is in the marketplace, where we have been bought with a price, as a slave in a slave market—redemption. Then the third picture connects us to a courtroom, and is the positive counterpart to our redemption, whereby innocence has been imputed to us despite our guilty hearts and deeds—justification. It's the opposite of condemnation, what Martin Luther considered "the principal article of all Christian doctrine, which maketh true Christians indeed."[59] Justification by faith rather than works, and all it entails, is what gave rise to the Protestant Reformation and turned the Christian world upside down. Revisiting what justification in Christ means for Christians is challenging, because it flies in the face of how most people understand the world works. In fact, it's one of the primary doctrines that sets Christianity apart from all other religions. The fourth picture from Stott illustrates the achievement of the cross, and concerns the home, with the family—reconciliation.

Many evangelistic methods rightly have an initial focus on explaining the two initial things the Cross accomplished for the salvation of those who believe, propitiation and redemption. They explain the seriousness of sin, blood sacrifice, and how God's anger must be averted in order for Him to show his love. He pays a price for sin's debt that no one else could pay, to buy individuals and free them from slavery to sin. But these two concepts are unique to the way that God interacts with us and not something that we generally do for others. No earthly person needs to officially have their righteous anger assuaged in order for them to love others, and individuals aren't able to buy and redeem others from their sin. Most evangelistic and discipleship methods focus on understanding these concepts in order to bring about thankfulness for what God has done, in part to motivate people to live differently. It's essential that we understand and grasp the power of propitiation, redemption, and justification as described above. But there's more to it than this. These concepts must be embraced for salvation, but not necessarily as a guide for what we do next. Yes, there are some early steps in our Christian lives that can serve as visible proof of our commitment to Christ, but our long-term discipleship should not simply be obedience-or-works-based. Rather, one could argue that justification, fully understood, involves our realization that being "born again" (the necessity of which Christ explained to Nicodemus in John 3) is a matter of the repentant and trusting heart before God, and not the acclaim of fellow men. Yes, we can care for our reputations and the impressions and feeling of others, but we no longer tie our worth to their opinions. For, at the highest level, we are answerable only to Christ, who has redeemed and altered us for himself.

By reconciliation through the cross, God has assembled and is assembling a family of faith in a world shattered not only by Adam's sin, but by ours also. In discipleship training, new believers grow in their understanding of God as their Father, and how he is closer to them than most people would have ever thought. He guides believers as his children, as those who stand to inherit everything: "Thus, reconciliation, peace with God (atonement), adoption into his family and access into his presence all bear witness to the same new relationship into which God has brought us."[60] But until we truly understand justification, we can be disgruntled children (Lk 15:28-32). Justification in Christ should ideally create a person who no longer craves recognition from others and who no longer feels as though they need to prove themselves, so they can finally rest from this striving, and hear with more and more clarity what God is calling them to be and do. Then they are able to live life as a child who has been truly reconciled to his Father, no longer fighting against him, but relying on him, trusting him and learning to hear his voice. This is where believers learn to abide in Christ and walk in the Spirit, which you might call the more supernatural or mystical side of the Christian faith.

Learning to get a handle on what it means for believers to live as those justified by Christ, which is a primary focus of this book, does sometimes require good old-fashioned hard work at self-denial and biting our tongue, but this is all a means to an end. Unlike Buddhism, where suppressing desire is what brings about a happy life, Christians believe that "crucifying themselves" and "considering others better than themselves" is only truly satisfying if it results in closeness to the One who created them and it brings him glory. (Witness Paul's counsel to slaves in Titus 2:9-10, that their response to the masters' directions should be pleasingly cooperative, respectful, and trustworthy "so that in everything they may adorn the doctrine of God our Savior.")

The Holy Spirit truly works through those who learn to rely on the Lord and grow in their dependence on Him. The "peace that passeth all understanding" is not just a result of trusting in the Lord with our mind and our heart; it also concerns the work of the Spirit of the Lord, who comes close to those who rely on him and trust in him through Christ. But telling ourselves or someone else to just get closer to God is easier said than done. And we have all met people who claim to be close to God, but have a "closeness" that is suspect and often detached from any widely accepted spiritual truth. There are also times that believers want time to "pray about a decision," whose right answer seems pretty obvious to others, with the hope that whatever decision they make will be accepted without criticism or probing questions because they claim to have prayed about it. Of course, we should pray without ceasing, but this does not mean that whatever we come up with during our times of prayer are from the Lord.

Some of the concepts in this guide can be a tool to evaluate what we hear the Lord telling us when we pray, to help us see if it passes the sniff test as something from the Lord, and not just something we want to do with a spiritual coating. The ultimate goal of this guide is for the reader to experience greater spiritual intimacy with God, as a friend, Father, and ever-present help, by showing us how our inability to see ourselves, and our tendency to deceive ourselves and self-sabotage our spiritual growth, is often our greatest obstacle in our progress towards this goal. Our understanding of justification can very well have something to do with it.

In 1988, Brazilian novelist Paulo Coelho published what proved to be a popular allegory, *The Alchemist*.[61] It pictures an Andalusian shepherd boy, Santiago, who undertakes a quest (to visit the Pyramids) that came to him in a dream. The journey is fraught with unforeseen challenges and astonishments, but Coelho portrays the universe as "conspiring" to move Santiago along to the fulfilment of his dream. On the Christian model, our dream is the realization of God's calling for our lives, and the universe is the Lord's sovereign watch care, whereby he makes us more like him by making us more dependent on him. As with Santiago, we may find our dream fulfilled closer to home than we imagined, but, whatever the course, we are changed by the journey, and our treasure cannot just be measured by what we happen upon at our destination (heaven). The path that God has for us is more about his forming us into who he wants us to be as we learn to rely on him and hear his voice.

In summary, if the four pictures of what Christ accomplished at the Cross are framed as a guide to the path of our Christian life, Propitiation and Redemption are the more technical side of that achievement. We must surely understand, believe, and accept this. Justification is the technical side of how this is applied to us now, as we give up on trying to earn salvation, we surrender ourselves, and we trust in him by faith. Justification is not just a concept to understand and appreciate like propitiation and redemption, but it is one that plays out in the way that we think of ourselves, treat others, and see God. As John Piper explains in his book *Providence*, "The key to killing sin and pursuing holiness, in a way that does not contradict justification by faith, is to realize that the only sin that can be successfully killed is forgiven sin. And the only lived-out holiness that pleases God is the holiness we pursue because we are already holy."[62] Once we have a right view of propitiation, redemption, and justification, we can live in the light of true reconciliation with God, growing as sons and daughters in the family of God, as those who are set to inherit what has been prepared for us. But the lynchpin that seems to unlock true victory in Jesus is how we understand Justification by Faith, which is the primary theme that ties this discipleship material together, and that it hopes to clarify.

CHAPTER 13

Our Will and Our Heart

The work that Christ does in the heart of believers is often difficult to identify and measure, but it is important that we be able to do so in order to know the direction we should head to become more like Christ. This is important in our own lives and in the relationships we have with other Christians so that we can enhance each other "as iron sharpens iron" (Proverbs 27:17). More mature Christians should be able to spot obstacles and misunderstandings in the lives of new believers so they can help guide them, and thereby understand more about themselves as well. One thing I hope they'll see is that believers in Christ actually have an even purer free will than Adam, and grasping this can help them live less defeated lives. God's plan was to take his children to a higher spiritual plane than Adam enjoyed. The Lord didn't initiate salvation history after the Fall just to get us back to the original state of Adam. Building on this truth, I hope to show that we ourselves are the biggest hindrance in our quest for fruitful discipleship.

The focus of this discussion is on a practical level in the lives of believers, upon what type of understanding we should have regarding our faith, so that we might become more like Christ. There are two core contexts that we need to see clearly in order to move towards becoming the people God wants us to be. The first concerns why we choose to follow Christ, and the second is how we follow Christ. When we decide to surrender our lives to him, we need to see ourselves clearly, and know that we are sinful (wrong) at our core, consistently disregarding and defying the Will of God, and that we can do nothing to make this right. Only God can show this to us, for we are blinded to this truth until he reveals it. Seeing our bleak situation clearly, and hearing the Good News of what Christ has done, we're left with no real option than to surrender ourselves to God through Christ. This surrender should be made to God because of who he is and what he has done; it's not based upon our desire for power, comfort, health, or wealth. And insofar as this discussion pertains to those of us professing faith in Christ, it provides a way to evaluate the extent and purity of our surrender, providing a guide to what we should be pursuing as Christians. Of course, in Matthew 5:12 and 6:19-21, Jesus promises a "great reward" in heaven for those persecuted on his account and urges us to "lay up treasures in heaven." A variety of verses pick up on this theme, so there is a place to anticipate eternal benefits to a consecrated life. But this is a far cry from calculating earthly benefits and advantages based on discipleship. In fact, that's the exact opposite of what we should be thinking.

The second thing we need to see clearly is that we are justified (or made right) in Christ because God has made it so and has said we are, not because of anything we have done or will do. This does not mean that everything we do is right (or anything we do is right, for that matter), but, rather that, when all is said and done, we have been made acceptable, even blameless, to God through Christ. This should affect every situation that deals with right and wrong in our lives. At a core (or primal) level, God has established and declared us as beings in right standing with him in Christ. All of us (including Adam) want to be right (justified) when we have done wrong, whether these things are big or small. This desire, and not just the initial sin itself, is understandable, but potentially dangerous. It can go very wrong and control us, wreaking spiritual damage. It is difficult to judge a Christian's life based on how much good and bad that they do, but it is easier to see how they respond when accused of being wrong, whether by themselves or by others.

Adam and Eve immediately started blaming others instead of admitting they were wrong, and just a few moments before this, they were unspoiled humans, untainted by sin. But there was still a level of innocence and confusion about the shame they felt after sin. This did not last long. The next chapter we hear how Cain immediately became angry when his offering was not well regarded by God after the first act of worship recorded in the Bible. God addressed this anger, "If you do not do what is right, sin is crouching at the door. Its desire is for you, but you must rule over it" (Genesis 4:7 NIV). The hardness that we have in our hearts when we are told that we are wrong is often similar to Cain's. The text does not tell us why Cain's sacrifice was not accepted, but God immediately addressed what was going on in Cain's heart. He didn't say the sacrifice was sin (even though it could have been); he said that when we do wrong, sin is crouching at our door. This sin that wants to overcome us is found at least as much, if not more, in what we do after we sin or are accused of sinning. Cain immediately took premeditated action to murder his brother Abel, which was far worse than his inappropriate sacrifice. In a similar way David, after his sin with Bathsheba, went on to deceive and try to manipulate Uriah before murdering him (2 Samuel 11-12). This was much more premeditated and evil than his initially impulsive sin of adultery. In a similar way, the Pharisees' primary concern with outward appearances and the letter of the law could have been resolved simply with repentance, but the righteous actions of Jesus convicted their hearts to such an extent that they resolved to murder Him. They failed to heed the sin that was crouching at their door, and they had no way to control it.

In each of these cases, an initial sin set the stage for commission of an even graver sin. These violent responses to accusations and/or internal convictions of wrongdoing sometimes take the form of abuse toward others who have nothing to do with the accusation. When we do evil, one of our natural inclinations is to attack those we see as more righteous (1 John 3:11-15). But the justification of Christ in our lives should free us from such follow-up sin. Still, so much in us rebels against admitting our sin. If we truly believe and concede we are wrong in the little things, there is something in us that believes it is a crack in the dam that will bring everything that we are and have crumbling down, so we need to protect ourselves against insisting that we're always right as if our life depended upon it. Again, once we truly believe we are justified in Christ at a core level, then we don't feel threatened by being shown wrong in the little (and big) things and can see each situation clearly for the first time. We do not have to ultimately justify ourselves. If we are wrong, we should eventually be able to see it every time, and if we are criticized, we should be able to receive the criticism without toxic emotion and learn what we can from it. Thus, we see developing maturity in the heart of a believer, whether in ourselves or in others.

This core justification in Christ should allow Christians to see how they are right or wrong in the many decisions they make each day, their minds and hearts not clouded by the idea that they have to be right. Of course, this can be an ongoing challenge for us Christians, because even though the moment we accept Christ, we admit we are wrong without excuse, we then start thinking we have to be right again (because we have been made right) and fall back on our perceived obedience to the Law of God as our guide. We develop a sense of pride and look down on unbelievers (and even on other believers) instead of maintaining a humility that should go to the core of who we are, with a new, born-again nature that allows us "to consider others as better than ourselves." This sober look at our own sinfulness does not need to be depressing. Rather, it's a blessing to finally grasp who we are – flawed beings, prone to stumble and disappoint in a messed-up world – while having an ongoing hope that what God is doing in our lives through Christ will make us better disciples.

The subtly different, but vastly important, advantage that believers in Christ have over the "free will" of Adam is that we don't have the burden of always being in the tenuous position of failing to keep the law of God. Adam always had to prove (justify) himself in order to truly be in right relationship with God. But this struggle to justify ourselves is a losing battle, and Christianity provides the only real answer to our ongoing sin and how to be right with God.

Yes, of course, there is a time to set the record straight when we're being slandered. Paul did as much in 2 Corinthians. And yes, there is a time to stand up for critical doctrines of the faith, even as here we plant our flag for the cause of salvation by grace, not works. But our self-justification mechanism is hair triggered, prone to misfire and miss the target, greatly harming ourselves and others. And that is where we must direct our fresh and strong attention.

CHAPTER 14

Our Justification

As John Stott explained in *The Cross of Christ*, one thing Christ has done for us has legal connotations—justification. There are other passages of Scripture that use legal terms we can use to understand the position of men before God. For instance, in Philippians 3:20, Paul speaks of our "citizenship in heaven," and, as we read in Acts 16 and 22, he was keenly aware of the importance of citizenship as he appealed to his rights as a Roman citizen. Also, when he speaks of the Christian's "spirit of adoption" in Romans 8:15, his usage was informed by the Roman institution of civil adoption, in which the one adopted is necessarily desired, a factor not always the case with physical sonship.

As for justification, imagine that you are in a courtroom, but without a jury or opposing lawyers —what we sometimes call a "bench trial." You are, indeed, on trial, and God/Jesus is the Judge (Romans 14:10-12). You have decided to represent yourself, so you are your own lawyer. The one accusing you is Moses, who represents the Law of God (John 5:45). So how shall you handle your own case? God has offered us a plea bargain: If we will plead guilty to violating his Law, as charged by Moses, then he will count what he did on the cross as our verdict and punishment, and we will be free of the burden of justifying ourselves before him. But most people just cannot accept that deal for a variety of reasons and so they try to argue their case before God. Every day, those who have not accepted the plea deal of admitting their guilt and putting the verdict in God's hands feel as though they are on trial to prove themselves before God. And they are.

Our pursuit of being justified (considered right) in how we think and choose impacts almost all of the relationships in our lives, whether with God and men, or within ourselves. We typically rationalize and try to justify all the decisions we make in life no matter how wrong they actually are, and we get defensive if people question us. Then we attack and criticize others because they do not do things the way we think they should, feeling that they need to justify their decisions to us before we can accept them. We want recognition and affirmation from others because they are helping us feel justified and respected. Furthermore, we have trouble accepting negative things that come our way and sometimes demand that God justify his decisions to us. If we don't understand the reasons, we usually don't accept them. Even seemingly honorable attempts at theodicy—seeking to explain how God can allow evil in the world, and defending him—put him in the position of needing to justify himself to us. We also have trouble living with ourselves if we aren't successful, or if we don't feel as though our lives are full of meaning. If we fear that our lives are fruitless, we strive internally to justify who we are, where we are, and how we spend our time. And our discontent leads us to lash out at others as we try to convince them to agree with us. Those two forces—our need to feel justified, and our insistence on justifying others (including God)—affects most aspects of our lives.

As those who are "made right" in Christ, we become even more concerned with what is right and wrong when we surrender ourselves to Christ. While this can be good for a variety of reasons, God is not going to use our concern with right and wrong to work the most important things in our personal lives. We can use concern with being right to justify all kinds of evil in the way we interact with others. On a light note, this can be seen in something as simple as siblings "getting back at each other" when someone wasn't "fair." Domestic abuse of children and spouses are often more serious examples of this sort of thing, where a perceived offense by one member of the family is met with an emotional tongue lashing meant to demean or even with a physical blow. Or in the political arena, if a politician makes a mistake in his personal life, it can be used to destroy him and his family. The same can happen to a pastor who has a moral failure in ministry. Illicit behavior deserves punishment, and it usually makes a pastor unfit to lead, but that does not mean that he and everyone he knows deserve endless and far-reaching chastisement for life. Each situation is different, but it is easy to go too far when meting out "justice" to others. Just as the Law of God is good, but can be an obstacle to our receiving righteousness in Christ, our concern with being right is good, but is potentially an obstacle to becoming like Christ. The story of how Jesus treated the adulteress comes to mind (John 8:1-11).

A clearer way to see where we are in our spiritual maturity is to focus on how we react and interact with others when we do wrong (or less than the best), or even when we are unfairly accused of doing wrong. This is where we can see if we understand ourselves to be on trial before God just like everyone else and whether we are still acting as our own lawyers rather than take the plea deal. And the thing about the plea deal is that everyone else knows the contents of the deal. We can't keep it secret that we have pleaded guilty to everything. Everyone else knows we are just as guilty as they are. That's why Jesus tells us not to render summary judgments on others (Matthew 7:1-5), because we are the accused and have never been in the position of authoritative magistrates. This doesn't mean we can't tell when something is wrong and confront others about it; it just means that we shouldn't let ourselves start to think that we are the judges. Indeed, we can be as illegitimate as crooked lawyers when we make dismissive judgments.

It seems as though we could use reason to make solid moral judgments, but the problem is that this drive to get what we want and to feel justified is so powerful that we often put all the powers of our reasoning at its service. We would like to think that it makes sense that, because we are doing the best we can and are pretty good compared to others, God should allow us into heaven. No book of Scripture tells us to do what we think is right and it will be okay, but most of us think we will be okay on these grounds. Even some of the most evil acts in human history seemed the right thing to do to those doing them. The problem is that when we are clouded by sin, we don't see things as they truly are. We call good things bad, and bad things good.

In *Righteous Minds*, Jonathan Haidt compares the workings of our minds and hearts when we make decisions to the fortunes of a man sitting on the back of an elephant. When we hear something, we usually draw our conclusions in a few seconds because that is what our heart and intuition tell us. This is the elephant, going wherever it wants to go. Subsequently, we bring to bear all of our education, rational arguments, and passion to support what we have already made up our minds to do—the workings of the man. The elephant is much more powerful, so we're typically not inclined to step back with a clean slate and rationally decide what to do. Our education and intellectual capacities are often used to justify what we want or what we believe intuitively.[63] Not only this, but we can "lie, cheat, and justify so well that we honestly believe we are honest." We are more like crooked lawyers in the way that we use reason, instead of the ideal of a scientist who "objectively" seeks truth, whatever the implications of the conclusion.

This is not to say we must stop to ponder the choices involved in every decision we make. Without snap judgments, we'd be paralyzed or harmed. If a car jacker in a ski mask and with a gun makes a run toward us at a stop sign, we shouldn't pause to ponder whether he's just a poor fellow needing a ride. When we smell something suspicious in an email telling us to download a file, we're quite reasonable in passing on that offer. But there is also peril in living strictly by quick takes. You'll miss out on some wisdom and angles you would have gained if you'd just stepped back and given it some thought. And it shouldn't be make-believe thoughtfulness, the sort where you're immune to good points you need to hear. Otherwise, you're just riding along on the old elephant. And on many occasions, it's prudent to register your intuitions in pencil rather than ink, amenable to erasure and rewrite should serious discussion and further consideration lead you in that direction.

Here's an example: For the LGBT community, being free to live how they want is not enough; they want everyone to agree with them (so they can feel justified), and they demonize others who don't agree with them (making others justify themselves to them). And another: On social media we want our voices to be heard in our comments (so we might feel justified), and if people attack us or our positions, our tempers flare since we are not at peace with others' justifying themselves at our expense. Also, if we have put a lot of work into something, and it is not recognized and acknowledged by others, we are usually on edge and ready to lash out because we don't feel recognized and we need that to feel justified in the work we did. At the same time, if we know that other people didn't put in the same amount of work on something as we did, yet they want to enjoy the results, we want to withhold the benefits of our work from them because they didn't earn them. Or we think we may treat them disrespectfully or harshly because they owe us something. The parable of the little red hen comes to mind. She did all the work, and no one helped her, so she selfishly enjoyed the bread alone. She used the good work that she did in making the bread to argue that she should be selfish. On the contrary, God says we should put others before ourselves and treat them as we would want to be treated. Trying to justify ourselves and our decisions will not get us there. Our whole lives are clouded with our desire and striving to be justified, but in vain. We may feel justified in small things, but there is no true justification for us except through Christ, and this realization changes us.

For those of us in Christ, this can still be a struggle. For even after we have been justified by Christ, it can take us a lifetime to internalize what it truly means to live in the light of the freedom it brings. Salvific justification in Christ is unique to Christianity, yet we seem to find it hard to fully receive the justification that God imputes (or ascribes) to us. As believers we become concerned with many noble causes such as reaching the world for Christ, and standing up for what is right, but we have a difficult time in our marriages and with certain people in our church. Our lives are littered with pain, unnecessary complications, and broken relationships. As Dostoevsky once wrote (in *The Brothers Karamazov*), "The more I love humanity in general, the less I love man in particular. In my dreams, I often make plans for the service of humanity, and perhaps I might actually face crucifixion if it were suddenly necessary. Yet I am incapable of living in the same room with anyone for two days together." These Seven Levels are an attempt to give believers tangible steps towards being able to live in the same room with someone for two days and interact with people throughout their lives. Each level is based on fundamental concepts that God is trying to teach us and toward which He is trying to move us.

We should not be overly concerned if others know our struggles, because they are not the judges, but just fellow crooked lawyers. Some are more crooked than others, but almost everyone can teach us something about ourselves. So, we should at least be able to listen to the advice of others and learn to count conflict and differences of opinion as tools God uses to take us to higher levels. He is always up to something in the lives of those who know they are guilty and have surrendered to Him.

CHAPTER 15

Matters of Conscience

A s we work through the way that we should interact with others when there is disagreement, things become more complicated when violations of God's clear commands are involved. If it is something that we have done, then we are probably not going to be open to discussing it with others because it could threaten to negatively affect many aspects of our lives. These discussions are often too volatile and too threatening to the vulnerable to make productive headway, and we would never interact with mere acquaintances about these issues. If it concerns the blatant sin of others, then, in certain situations we could have a responsibility as fellow Christians to confront them according to the procedure laid out by Jesus in Matthew 18:15-20. Of course, we should ensure we have the right heart when doing this. But we shouldn't forget that the Bible makes it clear that there is a time and place to bring rebuke and even exercise discipline when the sin is unmistakable. But "matters of conscience" are another thing, and it is here that these Seven Levels are best employed to evaluate how we should interact with others on difficult issues that we care about.

In Scripture, we find several lists of the deeds of the flesh with comparison to the deeds of the Spirit. And, to be sure, these deeds of the flesh are wrong regardless of the intentions of a person's heart. But most of the arguments and disputes we are comfortable to enter concern cloudier issues, "matters of conscience," which can be the source of serious conflict within churches, marriages, and families. They can even separate close friends and lead to feuds that last for generations. Some of the more absurd sounding examples that come to mind are the color of the carpet in church renovations, what worship music to use in a service, and what restaurant to patronize on a date. But when we are locked in arguments surrounding these issues, they don't seem absurd at all. That's because there are deeper issues at play.

There were also significant matters of conscience during biblical times. Paul dealt with several, including whether or not to eat food sacrificed to idols, what "holy" days to celebrate, and even the need of circumcision for non-Jews. Romans 14 provides several principles to guide us in how to make decisions and act when these conflicts arise. Before looking at them, keep in mind the strong urge we each have to declare what is right on every matter. On this account, it's easy to deceive ourselves and others about what issues are actually in play when we accuse others and defend ourselves. It is easy for us to tie larger theological issues to some of these "matters of conscience" in an effort to justify how passionately (or angrily) we fight for them. We always need to try to step back from ourselves, empathize with others, and see what core issue is really being discussed. We should be careful to allow God to work in the lives of others to convince them of what they should do pertaining to matters of conscience.

In this connection, we will look at a couple of examples in the life of Paul, and we will see that the theological issues that fired Paul up the most were those that threatened to limit the freedom that the gospel brings. He publicly shamed Peter for allowing his past habits and old way of thinking to negatively influence others and thus threaten the unity of believers. Any time we are tempted to judge others on matters of conscience, we should remind ourselves of the gospel first and who it is to which that we are each responsible. God judges each of us on many of these issues depending on what we personally think about them and how we respond, not necessarily on the issue itself. In many cases these matters of conscience are subjective, and God tells us how we should resolve them.

In Romans 14:1-15:7 we learn that:

1. There are those who are stronger in their faith than others. Paul considered himself as one strong in the faith, in large part because he believed that many matters of conscience can be allowed for those who are in Christ (Romans 14:14). The things that are outside of us are not nearly as important as what comes out of us (Mark 7:18-23).

2. That which makes things unclean are the thoughts of individuals about those things. For example, the same piece of food could be "unclean" for one person, but "clean" for another person. The uncleanness is not in the object itself.

3. We are not judges who determine what is clean or unclean for another person. We should focus on our own hearts, because that is what concerns God when He judges us. If we do not accept the actions of others when they are acting in accordance with their consciences, then it is as if we were setting ourselves up as having a higher standard than God (Romans 14:10). If God accepts them, how could we not (Acts 10:15)? And even if they were doing wrong, could God not handle them without our "help"? Of course, politely offering friendly advice may be helpful.

4. In matters of conscience, we should decide what is right for us by determining what we feel brings the most glory to God, as well as promotes peace among our brothers and sisters in Christ and adds to their spiritual edification (Romans 14:16-19). I hope this guide helps us to know the direction God wants to take us in our spiritual development, especially in the way we relate to others.

5. We should do what we really believe is right in our own heart. And if we are strong in our faith, our actions should show that we respect believers who've made different choices and that we're not out to destroy the peace in their hearts concerning what they think God wants them to do. We should not force others to follow our conscience, and we should not reflexively bend to other people's consciences if we believe differently. Yes, there are times when, out of tenderness, we defer to others' sensitivities, but we do not thereby surrender our freedom in Christ or signal that we recognize the tyranny of another's intrusive conscience.

Of course, there are cases when we are under authority, so that we will need to follow the leading of those over us concerning these matters of conscience, but the heart of the one leading and the one being led ideally line up with the aforementioned principles. This is also difficult in interactions between believers from different cultures and from different countries. In my context that means Indonesian Christians from traditional Christian, Catholic, Muslim, Hindu, and Buddhist backgrounds interacting as brothers and sisters in Christ, as well as with Western Christians. The struggles in unity for Christians from these different backgrounds often deal with matters of conscience and how we treat one another. We should take advantage of these opportunities to learn more about ourselves by interacting, leading, being led, and being open to criticism from those very different than us. By this, we can see ourselves more clearly and make headway up through the levels of Christian maturity.

There are two examples in the book of Acts where we see Paul interacting with others about a matter of conscience important to the Jews, circumcision. This will help illustrate how the issue of circumcision wasn't actually the core issue in these discussions, but it was more about the consciences of those involved. In Galatians 2:11-14, Paul relates the story of how Peter, who really believed that it was fine to eat with uncircumcised Gentiles because of Christ, then felt peer pressure to leave the Gentile believers and sit with James and other Jews. This situation is said to have confused some believers (including Barnabas) and left those who observed it start to have doubts about whether the gospel was powerful enough to allow this violation of Jewish law. Paul became very frustrated with Peter's indiscretion, and publicly shamed him—not because of the actual issue of circumcision, but because Peter acted in a way that violated his own conscience and began to disturb the peace and conscience of others. In this instance, Paul himself was disrupting the peace of others (specifically Peter), deeming this appropriate because of its importance: Peter was very influential, and this incident caused some confusion about a core issue of the gospel, the freedom of conscience we should have in Christ.

In contrast, in Acts 16:1-3, we see later that Paul actually told one of his closest partners in the gospel, Timothy, that he should be circumcised. How could it be that Paul would tell Timothy to be circumcised when he was free not to be, in Christ? It had to do with removing obstacles to being received by Jews in Greece (a matter related to peace with and empathy for others). So, we see Paul reacting emotionally against circumcision in one instance, and then actually encouraging it in another instance. The issue was not about circumcision, but about the conscience, peace with others, and a core issue of the gospel. How we interact with others and act in accordance with our conscience is a key to understanding our own hearts better.

In order to further narrow the breadth of these matters of conscience, these discussions on matters of conscience are most clear when they deal with issues between believers regarding their personal lives and the life of a local church, and not with government policies or individual views of the role of government in our lives. For example, if a believer thinks that the word to the people of Israel in Exodus 23:9 (to "not oppress a foreigner") requires all Christians to support a certain immigration policy, then they are mixing two different issues. The concern with "matters of conscience" on this issue would apply to the way immigrants were treated as neighbors or church visitors. If this belief stretches into requiring all other "true" Christians to support open borders or some other immigration issue, then that would be an attempt to limit their freedom to follow their conscience and the leading of the Spirit. Whether a modern secular government should align itself with the policies of a theocracy from thousands of years ago, and not follow its strategic and security objectives, is another issue.

These matters of conscience are also more difficult to discuss with unbelievers, because the very foundation of how we decide to do what is right is different. Everyone outside of Christ thinks that doing their best and following their conscience is how to live a good life. Christians operate from the core belief that every part of who we are has been corrupted by our pride and willfulness, and only when we give up trying to prove ourselves to God and admit we deserve death can God start to make us into what He wants us to be. Believers should always be the quickest to realize that we could be wrong, and then to be able to see things clearly. Furthermore, humility should be one of our most distinguishing marks. If not, these levels should help guide us.

I hope this book provides a useful framework for approaching examples from our daily lives, ones that can be evaluated to see how we can move in the direction God wants us to travel as Christians. We began with a look at the role the truth of the cross should play in our lives as believers. Next was an explanation of how our will and our heart are at the core of what God wants to accomplish in our lives. Then, we saw how our attempt at justifying ourselves is one of our core problems, and our justification is one of God's core accomplishments through Christ. In this chapter, we saw how matters of conscience are the easiest tools we have to work with when discussing these issues with others as well as receiving criticism from others. All of these concepts prepare us to understand how to identify our spiritual challenges as well as the struggles of others. I hope this will be something that can give us handles to work with as we try to steer ourselves, and one another, in the direction God wants us to head. And in the spirit of promoting unity among believers, I hope that these tools can be equally helpful to all believers, regardless of religious background.

CHAPTER 16

Our Direction as Believers

Evangelicals historically and properly put great emphasis on evangelism, with biblical admonitions to witness, from the Ascension—"in Jerusalem and in all Judea and Samaria, and to the end of the earth" (Acts 1:8)—to the last chapter of Revelation—"And let the one who hears say, 'Come'" (Revelation 22:17). Indeed, the words 'evangelical' and 'evangelism' share the Greek root for "good news," which we're to spread abroad in the conviction that there is a momentous divide between the lost and the saved, and that we need to be active in leading non-believers across that divide to Christ. But the Great Commission (Matthew 28:19-20) cautions us against thinking that our work is done once we've shared our faith, and, ideally, gotten a positive response. The key lies in "making disciples." This focus keeps us accountable to grow in our faith personally, along with any younger believers we are discipling, so we are all working together to become more like Christ. If we think the most important thing we can do in our lives is to sincerely say "Yes" to a gospel presentation, then it is easy to become disillusioned with Christianity and to lose direction in our walk with Christ. After all, if we've been saved and will spend eternity in heaven, what else is there? Well, there's a lot more that God wants to accomplish in our lives here on earth, and these are the things that actually require work on our part. The Bible tells us that we come to faith in Christ because God draws us to Himself and opens our eyes and heart, so that isn't something we achieve through our own efforts. The humility and surrender that is such an important part of being born again puts us in the state of mind and heart to start to become actual disciples of Christ. Being made into a disciple is a lifelong process, and something we need to work at under the guidance of the Holy Spirit. This path of becoming a disciple of Christ has goals and a certain direction we should be able to identify and evaluate, especially in our own lives, and to a certain extent, in the lives of others.

The following material should help narrow our focus in this connection and introduce some fundamental considerations regarding what God is desiring to do in our lives; what Christ has already done in our lives, something that's hard for us to accept; and how we can focus on smaller issues, so that we might better understand larger things about how we are (or are not) becoming more like Christ. While we share our faith with others and wait to see whose heart God will give understanding, we should always be striving alongside fellow believers to become disciples of Christ. This is not a theoretical exercise, but a very practical one that will show itself in the small, daily interactions we have with others. At the center of the issue is how we as disciples of Christ are to "be transformed by the renewal of your mind, that by testing you may discern what is the will of God, what is good and acceptable and perfect" (Romans 12:2). Our focus should be on what God wants us to do and what He is teaching us. This will take us in many different directions in life, as God guides us along our unique paths. He has something special in mind for all of us, and the point is not about getting what we want, but rather about being what God wants.

The following three chapters are designed to help us get into the Seven Levels for understanding the direction God wants to lead us. The first chapter—a short summary of the different levels—is followed by one that has seven daily devotionals which should help familiarize us with the concepts in each of the levels over the period of a week. Then the third and final chapter provides a detailed breakdown of these levels with Bible passages to ground and illuminate them. And so we have a framework to encourage strong focus on discipleship, one whose concepts are uniquely Christian. We should be increasingly amazed at how the suffering and death of Christ was not just something terrible that had to happen in the background of history to get us where we need to be, but rather something we should look at carefully to understand what God wants from us. These Seven Levels are based on Scripture passages, and I hope the biblical progression from 1 to 7 is clear. But the sequence isn't ironclad. You don't necessarily need to fully understand and live out one to move to another; they can work independently. But one would hope that they could be a general guide to deeper levels of understanding and life change in our walk with Christ.

The first two levels are beliefs we share with followers of the other Abrahamic religions, Judaism and Islam. While there will be some differences on the details, these teachings are not distinctively Christian. We might call them pre-conversion steps, necessary but not sufficient for salvation. Levels 3 and 4 are uniquely Christian, and if someone has accepted them, they can be considered a believer. Sad to say, someone who comes to Christ, may well return to a primary concern with Levels 1 (getting what we want) or 2 (the Law), but not in accordance with what they've learned about these levels in their journey to Christ. In effect, this puts them back where they were before Christ, albeit now framed in a spiritual way. So, they talk about how now they can follow the rules of the law and then get what they want through Christ. But one would hope that over time we will all start to move towards deeper understanding of what God desires for us in levels 5, 6, and 7. If a believer is more concerned with the content of Levels 1 and 2, it does not follow that they are not believers. (And yes, it's good that they seek to avoid murder, adultery, and stealing, as well as believe that God wants the best for them.) It just means that they are primarily concerned with the same things that Muslims and Jews might be concerned about and not the things that are distinctively Christian. Our struggles with general principles in levels 5, 6, and 7 can be seen in our social interaction with others, especially when it comes to "matters of the conscience." And when, in moments of disappointment, as with Cain when his sacrifice was not regarded by God, how we feel about certain situations is often written all over our faces (Genesis 4:5-6).

In level 5 we start to believe that others do not need to do what we want them to in order for us to relate with them positively. Then in level 6, we start to be at peace when others criticize us, whether fairly and unfairly. Finally, in level 7, we can start to live consistently with our justification in Christ (which actually took effect on level 3) and therefore choose to love God and others with all of our heart as a result of our newfound freedom.

Jesus sacrificed Himself to break the curse of sin and the unbearable weight of the Law so that we could be free from their power and truly please God. But living in light of this fact and learning to walk in the power of the Holy Spirit takes a lifetime. Unfortunately, it's possible to know the gospel and know Christ and still only operate in the realm of obedience out of fear and a desire to try to do the right thing in our own power. Learning to live in the light of grace and the power of trust and love is no small task, as that is counterintuitive to human reasoning in many ways. That is why many Christians do not truly understand how Jesus' surrendering himself and dying on the cross is a picture of how we should also live (Luke 9:23; Galatians 2:20). Many people do not understand how dependency and weakness can have power, and, indeed, how this posture is our only hope for pleasing God.

Paul speaks of spiritual milk and meat when he contrasts the Christian understanding of new believers (milk) with the insights of those who are more mature (meat). All followers of Christ have areas in their lives where they are more mature, as well as places of recurring struggle. We don't know what the thorn in Paul's flesh was, but it may have been something that posed little problem for other Christians. Each believer has special spiritual challenges, but, with the help of the Holy Spirit, every one of us should all be able to move forward in the process of becoming like Christ. And we should understand that becoming like Christ is not just about grasping concepts intellectually; it's indispensably about considering others more important than ourselves, about loving our enemies, about surrendering ourselves to God with a pure heart, and about being content in all situations. This can take a lifetime, and this Christian pursuit sets it apart from other religions. Christ taught that fearing God and following the rules are important, but that these things cannot change the hearts of men.

The hearts of men and women will always lead them astray, and, as Jesus explained regarding the Pharisees, they could follow even the most minute details of the law but be far from the will of God because of the condition of their hearts. Jesus let us know that if we even think about breaking a part of the law, we are guilty of breaking all of the law. Even more confounding is the fact that the very revelation of the perfect Law of God to mankind makes us sin even more. As Martin Luther explained in Thesis 1 of his Heidelberg Disputation, "The law of God, the most salutary doctrine of life, cannot advance humans on their way to righteousness, but rather hinders them."[64] Jesus was the only one who obeyed the Law of God successfully, so no one else is worthy to guide mankind in how to follow God with their whole heart. Don't forget how Jesus repeatedly condemned and offended those who thought they understood how obeying God pleased God, and whose overarching "ministry" was to pressure others to obey religious rules. He called them white-washed tombs and snakes because they were agents of spiritual poison and decay. It's easy to condemn the Pharisees and consider ourselves on the side of Jesus, but when left to our own devices, most of us revert to rule-following as the path to holiness. That is why we all need the community of Christ to help us in this journey.

If we think we are pleasing God with our actions and that we know what God wants from others, beware. We should regularly take time to evaluate ourselves and how our own hearts are attempting to lead us astray, especially if we think we are in a position to coach and lead others. We should also be attentive to how others view us, and be willing to accept criticism from others and hear what they are telling us. Most of the time there is some truth in what others say, and we would be remiss in ignoring it. This is especially true when the comments are coming from a fellow believer who thinks much differently from us. I'm sure the Pharisees commended each other, because they essentially thought alike, but if they had really listened to what the peasants thought of them, they might have learned something. It was no coincidence that God chose Mary and Joseph, those of low station, to raise the Son of God. He chose those who were humble in heart who would immediately believe and have faith in what He told them. Compare their response to the news of the coming Messiah with that of the Jewish priest Zechariah, who had his mouth immediately shut by God because of his doubt about the birth of John. We need to be able to discern what God is telling us through circumstances and through others even if it goes against our plans and how we think things should go. Indeed, the counsel of those who find fault in our thinking or acting may well put us on a better path. As Dallas Cowboys coach Tom Landry put it, his job was often one of "calling people to do what they don't want so they can become what they want to be." In writing about discipleship evangelism, Bill Hull enlisted that quote to illuminate a pastoral role, one that comes into play as believers shepherd one another. Proverbs 27:17 puts it this way: "Iron sharpens iron, and one man sharpens another."[65]

God does not leave us to struggle alone as He works in us, but He does allow our spiritual growth to be accompanied by some level of suffering. While evil in the world is the cause of much suffering, it is not the cause of all suffering. There are good things that cause us to suffer, and these are often times that we learn the most about ourselves. In the midst of suffering, we can see many things more clearly than before, and God uses it to accomplish His purposes. Just like Job's friends, when we aren't the ones suffering, we like to create theories about what is causing it, and it is often related to our works. But Job's suffering was not because of His sin, but because God allowed Satan to do it. Job, in the midst of his suffering, was not concerned with theories, but cried out to God as one totally dependent on Him. This is what God desires, and sometimes it takes suffering to get us there. Our loving God does not subject those he loves to suffering flippantly, for those who are in Christ were chosen before we were born, and he plans for us to be with him in eternity. He will see his work through to completion. And when we realize just how much we go astray, and how much we need him, he will leave the ninety-nine and come find us (Matthew 18:10-14).

Riches, power, and health are not reliable signs of our progress in the pursuit to become who God wants us to be, but rather we should look to humility of heart and a childlike dependence on God, along with a realization of who it is that we should truly fear and be beholden to. Becoming more childlike before God, while attempting to lead our own children, being humble while confidently leading others, and waiting on the Lord while struggling and striving in this world, all seem like contradictions and impossibilities. But this seemingly impossible pursuit to be who the Lord wants us to be—more like Christ—does have simple steps, even if fully understanding and applying them is still difficult. But it is a worthy pursuit, and these Seven Levels are an attempt to organize the teachings of the Bible into a framework to help us understand that path. During this journey, we must agree with Jesus that "he must increase, but I must decrease" (John 3:30), which will then allow us to better determine, and follow, the details of the individual path that God is laying out for us as "we work out your own salvation with fear and trembling" (Philippians 2:12).

Simple Summary of Levels

Level 1: One of our most important needs is to be justified.

Level 2: Our thoughts and actions deem us unworthy/ unjustified.

Level 3: If we believe we are unjustified, we can be justified by Christ.

Level 4: Christian acts of obedience do not justify our identity.

Level 5: The church teaches us how hard it is to stop judging others and requiring them to justify themselves for unity.

Level 6: We realize our justification in Christ releases us from our endless need to defend/prove ourselves and accuse others.

Level 7: With our newfound freedom, we choose to sacrifice things we want for others (love) with trusting dependence upon God.

CHAPTER 17

Seven Levels Summary

1. **Our most important needs are not health, safety, and prosperity, but the need to be considered justified in our decisions in the eyes of man and God.**
   Why would Jesus' forgiving sins and criticizing religious leaders enrage people enough to kill Him?

2. **By the measurements of religious law, we are all considered unworthy, and we are not justified in the decisions we have made in the eyes of either man or God. We must truly believe this.**
   Did any of the Old Testament prophets live sinless according to the Law of God, and, if not, why did God choose them and how did he consider them righteous? Do we really think we are good people?

3. **Only when we truly believe and admit that we are wrong/unjustified in the decisions we have made, and have no defense, and repent of our sinful thinking and acting, will God declare us justified. We are then born again as justified humans and have the potential to develop into genuine disciples of Christ.**
    What does it mean to obey the Law of God with a pure heart, and why couldn't we do it before Christ? Who could dispute the details of God's plan if they were truly throwing ourselves upon God's mercy?

4. **After we have been justified through Christ, we will often continue to try and justify ourselves in the eyes of man and God, but as we develop into disciples of Christ, our hearts and minds will be transformed.**
    Are there any circumstances when we should not truly forgive someone, and if so, what does that tell us about ourselves? Does obeying Christ require a detailed understanding of the Old Testament Law?

5. **The church is the context in which we learn that people of all races and backgrounds can be justified in Christ, and that they do not gain salvation from righteous behavior, group identity, or the approval of others.**
    Do we harbor any prejudices against believers of other races and nationalities, or those who are very different from us? Have we sacrificed anything or invested anything of value into the lives of fellow believers at our church? Do we believe that Jesus should be worshipped by all humanity?

6. For the sake of vital truth rather than mere personal vindication, Christ and his Apostles could be seen to set the record straight when false accusations were hurled at them, but we must understand that our saving justification in Christ should empower us to have peace when others seek to justify themselves, even when it is at our expense. Because we are free in respect to all, we make ourselves servants to all. This is the example of Christ.

   Do our emotions run high and we lash out in anger when others falsely (or fairly) accuse us of things? Is it possible for humans in their own power to have peace when others are attacking or hurting them?

7. When we truly understand in our hearts that we have been justified at our core by God through Christ (even though we are demonstrably unjustified according to the Law), we are finally able to live an unhindered, full life capable of pure trust and sacrifice with love and thankfulness. Justification sets us free to worship God in a way superior to that of Adam.

   Have you ever been in a situation where you saw no way out, and then someone you had gravely wronged in the past risked themselves to help you in a way you could never repay? And then after you survived that situation, that same person patiently and lovingly guided you to the truth even while you repeatedly made mistakes? Would you ever question that they loved you? How would you feel if they told you to do hard things?

CHAPTER 18

Seven Levels Devotional

Over a period of seven days, at the rate of one devotional a day, this document gives an introduction to the Seven Levels of understanding/discipleship that applies to the lives of all believers, regardless of background or nationality, to help us identify where we/they are and what direction we should be heading in our Christian lives.

Day 1. Level One – Luke 5:17-26

Read this passage and think about why Jesus would look at this crippled man and, then, the first thing that came out of His mouth was, "Be clean," instead of "Be healed. . . . Get up, pick up your mat, and go home." There could be several reasons, but since Jesus was aware of the faith of this man and his friends, he knew they were ready for something more important than physical healing, namely spiritual forgiveness. He then tells the Pharisees that he will cure this man to prove that he has the power to forgive sins.

The temporal power of Jesus to control the weather, cast out demons, heal the sick, raise the dead (Mk 4-5), and even forgive sins (Lk 7:36-50), was not central to his mission. The people Jesus touched would experience bad weather again; perhaps be possessed again; get sick again; and sin again. And in the three cases where he raised people from the dead, they would ultimately die again. Yes, the power of Jesus over these things is crucial to understand the extent of his power and how He cares for us, but going to Jesus for physical stuff we desire does not reflect spiritual depth. We get a clue to this as well in the parable of Lazarus and the Rich Man (Lk 16:19-31), where the eternal destiny of the affluent man was miserable and the inheritance of the man who was miserable on earth was glorious.

The concerns of this level preoccupy many, whether believers or unbelievers. It's here that people look for solutions to temporal problems, things like health and finances. Within Christianity, the "Health & Wealth" movement shows this most clearly, but most believers, whatever their denominational focus, pray frequently for these types of things. Muslims, Jews, and Hindus are also looking for blessings like this from a higher power. To be sure, there is nothing wrong with level one, but it is not distinctively Christian. Rather, it operates at the surface level. Things like spiritual forgiveness are more important, along with other heart issues; temporal solutions are not as pressing as eternal solutions. Of course, these matters are all interconnected, but we should spend time thinking about how much we prioritize level 1 concerns, which we share with even children, new believers, and nonbelievers.

Day 2. Level Two – 2 Samuel 7

Read this prophetic passage and think about all the history behind it and the vast future before it. Think about previous prophecies, such as those about crushing the serpent's head, blessing the whole world through the descendants of Abraham, redeeming and guiding Israel to the promised land, and then this one projecting an eternal kingdom in the house of David. These Old Testament prophecies affect all of mankind, and in this one to David, the word about discipline for disobedience is not just about light slaps on the wrist, but also extends to the exile of Israel and Judah to Assyria/Babylon/Persia. But God always redeems his people, and he also holds sway over the leaders of other nations to accomplish his purposes. At the time these prophecies and events were recorded, they provided clues that God was taking this world in a certain direction, and he chose through whom and how he wanted to work. He frustrated the expectations and desires of many. He didn't take sin lightly, he demanded blood for forgiveness, and it was on his timeline. Nothing could stop what he wanted to accomplish, and his focus was bigger than upon any one individual. Nevertheless, though the sweep of his work was enormous, indeed, comprehensive, he did not shy away from using the smallest and weakest of people, those who were surrendered to him and who trusted in him.

The past is important and gives weight, meaning, and strength to anything connected to it in the present and future. Though we shouldn't dwell on the past, it is nonetheless an important part of this world and who we are as humans. Our origins help us understand more about why we are here and who we answer to as our Designer. Interest, study, and even belief at this level in the Old Testament does not make someone a Christian; it's something that Jews and Muslims can accept as well. Perhaps Buddhists and Hindus would be interested in these stories, but they would probably have more problems with the specifics.

While believing stories and prophecies in the Old Testament does not make someone a follower of Christ, it does seem to reflect greater spirituality than is at play in level 1. At that level, we considered the contrasting fates of Lazarus and the Rich Man (Lk 16:19-31), but there's a level two lesson from that parable as well. Note that Abraham dismisses the Rich Man's request that someone come back from the dead to warn his relatives on earth. The reason for Abraham's response is that they already have the divine testimony and teaching of Moses and the prophets, which is greater in substance than whatever dazzling, miraculous phenomenon they might encounter. If they've turned their noses up at the former, there's no reason to think they'll turn to God in the face of the latter. As we grow in our understanding, we see that as God worked through specific people in a specific way, by specific acts and specific prophecies, yet all of this pointed to the specific, grand plan he had in mind for the entire world. Resolving the problem of mankind's sin was not a temporary or quick fix, but a long story marked with death, pain, and weakness (see also Isaiah 52-53, which traces God's work through the Hebrews' Egyptian captivity down through the centuries to the sacrifice of the Suffering Servant, Jesus, on the cross).

Take some time to think about the seriousness of sin in your own life, and notice that no matter how long you've been a believer, it still rears its ugly head. All humans should be able to identify with the recurring disobedience of Israel, and not look down on them, because their story is part of mankind's story. Think about God's patience and understanding in working with us, and all humans throughout history, even though He knows exactly who we are, and what our weaknesses are, even when we don't see them. It's a wonder that, despite all our sin, foolishness, and hardness of heart, he stands ready and willing to forgive the repentant (for more on this see: Ex 4:10-17; 2 Sm 12:1-25; Ps 51).

Day 3. Level Three – John 10

At this level, we identify individuals who understand the gospel and the choice that God's plan of salvation presses upon them. They start to deal with the fact that this is not just an intellectual decision to affirm the power of Christ and believe the accounts of His historical acts. It's more than this—a matter of surrender and life change. Here they build upon the content of Levels 1 and 2, which focused on the temporal power of Jesus and His concern with forgiveness and heart issues. These matters indicated that He was the Promised One God sent to carry out the eternal aspects of the plan which was unfolding throughout the Old Testament, its aim to create the true people of God.

Bible passages about the birth, life, death, and resurrection of Christ are included in this level, but even the demons believe these accounts. Clearly, it takes more than this to be a Christian.

Parables at this level include the Four Soils (Mk 4:1-20) and the Wheat and Tares (Mt 13:24-30, 36-43). Also drawing from the teaching about the Good Shepherd and the Cost of Discipleship in Luke 14:25-33, individuals should start to understand what kind of soil they are, whether they are wheat or tares (weeds), whether they are sheep whose shepherd is Christ, and whether they are ready to make a commitment. If they have reservations about whether what Christ has done is God's actual plan for salvation, his way to create his true people, then they aren't believers yet.

A local man whom a believer has been discipling for years is very knowledgeable about the Bible and considers himself a follower of Jesus. But he is still the soil where the worries of the world are choking out his ability to take steps of faith and truly commit to Christ. That's just where he is, and using parables helps us to specify his spiritual standing. This unbeliever has also mentioned the passage about the cost of discipleship in Luke 14:25-33, and he's doubtful that he's ready to start working on this "house" of Christian discipleship because he's not sure if he's ready to complete construction. If he weren't a Muslim, but rather a nominal Christian, we probably wouldn't doubt his salvation, because he would just blend in with all the church goers. He would have greater difficulty seeing what sort of soil he really was. The fact that he is from another faith allows him and us to see things a little clearer.

These levels are mainly about identifying where people are spiritually, which way they should be heading, and what building blocks are needed to undergird the higher levels. We don't really graduate from lower levels and we'll always need to return to them at certain points. At this level 3 and the next level 4, we are tempted to focus on our works to prove to ourselves and to others that we are children of God, but our salvation has never been about that. It's about believing in God's plan, accepting that Jesus is the fulfillment of that plan, and fully surrendering ourselves to Jesus as his sheep so that we can become a part of the people of God, able to hear his voice.

Take time to think about why you consider yourself a child of God even though there may be people you know who appear (and may actually be) living holier lives according to the Law, even as unbelievers.

Day 4. Level Four – John 14:15-27

Level 4 deals with the basic things that are expected of a Christian, the proper manner of life. This is where believers often focus. When they look at other believers, these are the observable things, so these practices can be taken, mistakenly, as totally defining Christianity.

When we give advice to others, it usually concerns these matters. Though they're issues of the heart, they also appeal to the mind, and so may be applications of the rational will. Consider these three parables: The Unforgiving Servant, in Matthew 18:21-35 (teaching the need to forgive as we are forgiven): The Rich Man, in Matthew 19:16-30 (on the need to follow Christ sacrificially, not weighed down by lower desires); and The Talents, in Matthew 25:14-30 (on devoting our gifts and resources to serve the Lord). Most believers will acknowledge these requirements, whether or not they satisfy them.

Of course, there are more marks of the believer: Evidence of new birth, a changed life (Jn 3:1-21); submission to baptism (Mt 3:11-17; Rom 6:1-11); accepting God's Word, the Bible (Mk 7:1-23; Acts 17:11; Rv 22:18-19; 2 Tm 3:15-17; Heb 4:12); engaging in prayer and fasting (Mk 1:35-45; Lk 6:12-19; Mt 6:5-18); assuming one's place in the church, the Body of Christ (Rom 12:3-21; 1 Cor 12:12-31; Acts 2:37-47); participating in the Lord's Supper (Jn 6:52-71; Lk 22:14-23, 1 Cor 11:23-34); and manifesting the primacy of love, obedience to Christ, and servanthood (1 Cor 13:1-13; Jn 14:15-27; Jn 13:1-20; Lk 22:24-27; Mt 20:20-28).

The variety of Scripture passages can give one the impression that the Christian life is simply a matter of ticking off things on a list, making sure all the behaviors are in order. Indeed, there are Christians throughout the world who think that employing these basic tools and modeling these life practices mark the end of their development to full Christian stature. Well, certainly, all believers need to attend continually to these things, but we all need to understand that the practices and lifestyles associated with this level are not ends in themselves. Rather, these tools are means toward progress to higher levels as the concept of love enlarges and deepens along the way.

Day 5. Level Five – Mark 1:16-20 and 3:31-5

Think about all the things you believe about the primacy of your family in your life, and then read these two passages again. Resist the urge to domesticate Jesus and explain away what He really means about the priority of the Kingdom. Think about two of his closest disciples' leaving their father in the boat when they went to follow Jesus. Think of Mary outside the house as Jesus brushes aside his earthly family and explains who his true brothers and sisters are.

I'm not going to try to make application to each situation. We each need to read what Jesus said and then consider how it might address our own family relationships.

This level tries to identify some real struggles that people of every culture have with being serious members of the family of God. And in our reflections, we need to revisit New Testament and Early Church teaching and practice, noting that those believers had a bond stronger than the blood ties of the biological family (Lk 14:26; 1 Cor 6:1-8).[66] And without even going that far, it is very difficult for some people to truly consider people from other cultures, people groups, and different religious backgrounds as their brothers and sisters in Christ. Think, for instance, about the level of connectedness each of you has with a local Indonesian congregation where you live. If you're not Indonesian by birth, do you really feel that you're a part of their larger Christian community as a brother or sister in Christ, or will your familial bond with other Westerners seem more compelling? How many Western Christians do you know who aren't even involved with a local Christian congregation and might be somewhat embarrassed to interact with traditional Indonesian Christians? Think about Muslim-background believers that you know. Do they have a hard time seeing themselves as the brothers and sisters of traditional Indonesian Christians? And what about those in traditional Indonesian churches? How would they receive a new Muslim-background believer who starts to move in their Christian circles, but who still looks like a Muslim and perhaps subconsciously considers himself better than the more mature Christians because of his scrupulously devout Muslim background? We can probably all identify with the relational difficulties involved with people of different cultures operating on a daily basis as the Body of Christ (including racially mixed congregations in the US).

An easier and early step in this direction is being faithful to the Great Commission and taking part in reaching out to people of other languages, tribes, and cultures, and conceding that we, when lost, were just as much in need of the gospel that we are now sharing with them (Rom 10:9-21; Mt 28:18-20; Acts 1-2). And, indeed, the saved need to continuously walk in the light and power of the gospel of grace that they proclaim to those they seek to reach. Living with the Family of God as a higher priority than any other relationships on earth is where the Lord wants things to head, and He wants us to consider other believers as brothers and sisters regardless of our race and culture.

The ministry of Paul showed the priority of planting churches among other cultures in early Christianity (Acts 9-10, 16-17, 19-20; 1 Thes 2-3; Col 2-3). The position of Christ above all the people of the world is also important and difficult for some to comprehend. Do most Christians think of Jesus as bringing the governments and businesses of the world under His authority and exerting his power over every aspect of our lives in the new world? Do they see Jesus as the Last Adam (Rom 5:8-21; 1 Cor 15:20-58), worshipped by Angels (Heb 1), our Forever Priest and Mediator (Heb 3; 7:23-28; 9:11-28), and the Word of God (Jn 1:1-29). At some level, most of us probably put Jesus in a corner of our lives, separated from "secular," cultural, or family issues, but he should actually be at the center of, and redefine, all of them. Our biases regarding church and what we believe about the more difficult commands of Christ can take a lifetime to sort out correctly.

What we think of the church and how we interact with it as members of the family of God provide clues to the extent we understand how we were chosen to be God's people, a Holy Priesthood (1 Pt 1:1-2:12). Making sacrifices to maintain healthy relationships with other people and to work through conflict is one of the most powerful forces God uses in our lives to make us more like Jesus, and such sacrifice should be common within the Bride of Christ (Eph 5:22-33; Rv 19:7-9). Our churches will be evaluated by the Lord, and there will be judgment (Rv 1-3; 20:11-15). Jesus will come again, riding on a white horse to bring the world as we know it to its knees (Rv 20; 22:6-21). He will bring about a New Earth where there is no more suffering and sorrow (Rv 7:9-17; 21-22:6) for the elect of God (Rom 8:28-10:4; 1 Thes 1). Is our local Family of God as important to us as Jesus wants it to be, and what are we doing about it?

Day 6. Level Six – Romans 7:7-25

How comfortable are you with losing or having someone take advantage of you? Are you able to take a step back for a moment and see how your wants and desires are the source of most of the grief and conflict in your life? In Romans 7, Paul explains that the Tenth Commandment is the one that killed him. We usually use the word "covet" when reciting this commandment, but we never use that word in our daily lives. A better way to think of it is "want" or "desire," and Paul knew that as a Pharisee zealous for the Law, he could manage commandments One through Nine but stumble at Ten. He realized that if he were judged on the righteousness of the wants of his heart, he would fail.

Of course, many wants are wholesome in themselves—wanting a drink of water on a hot day; a couple's desiring to have a child; hoping your car will get you home. But our desires can easily go astray when they turn to jealously and envy, willful indifference to God's leading and provision, erasure of gratitude for what he's given you, and a callous heart toward the needs of others, toward their legitimate wants, such as food for their children. And it is here that the Tenth Commandment cuts hard, leaving all of us without excuse.

The Sermon on the Mount (Mt 5:1-48) made this clear. If you even think about committing adultery, you are guilty. If you are angry with your brother, you are guilty of murder. So, not only do the desires of our hearts make us break the Tenth Commandment; they lie at the root of what leads us to break all of the other commandments. The Law does what it was designed to do, to show us that we are guilty and deserve death before God. There is no power of salvation in the Law, only guilt. So why are we humans so driven to prove our holiness by obeying the Law (or whatever religious teachings a person follows) when it always condemns us (Jn 5:44-45)? If we rebel against the Law, we are clearly in the wrong, but if we try to obey the Law in order to consider ourselves justified, are we not also trying to achieve a righteousness that we can use to prove to God that He should give us what we desire? Just like the Pharisees, we use our obedience to the Law as a weapon to show others (and God) how good we are and to keep away from an ongoing dependence on God. God asks us to die, not live our "Best Life Now," and, actually, only by dying do we live our "best life now."

The teachings of Martin Luther explain that there are two general ways that people understand mankind's path to God, the Way of Glory and the Way of the Cross. The Way of Glory says that we got a little off track in the Garden, but Jesus came to help us fix ourselves. We were perfect in the Garden and the Law and Jesus came to help us get back to that glorious state again. Almost all the religions of the world have a similar story, just as, at the end of Ramadan, Muslims are believed to return to the state of Adam (*fitri*). Similarly, Hindus and Buddhists suppress their desires in order to experience *moksha* and *nirvana*.

The Way of the Cross says something different: It says that no fix will remedy our problem as enemies of God (Rom 5:6-11). It tells it like it is; we all know that something is off and always will be with the hearts of men. Our hearts will always be driven by our selfish wants and desires, and, if we are made perfect again, just like Adam and Eve, we will fail again. The Way of the Cross demands that we die and allow God to make us into something new. We are a new creation, not like the one before, because we don't have to prove ourselves anymore; Jesus has already done that for us. We just need to die to ourselves and be totally dependent on God. We need to believe the unseen and that which we can't confirm when it comes from God (Lk 16:19-31; Heb 11; Rom 4). When our wants and desires do not line up with our current situation, we need to trust that God is providing exactly what we need (like our daily bread), and that He knows better than we do.

It is so hard for us to be content (Phil 4:11-13). In a world where marriage and family are seen as such an integral part of Christian culture, do we really believe that God calls some people to singleness so that they could better focus on the mission he has for them (1 Cor 7)? Many Christians would probably consider older single people as somewhat incomplete, but Paul says differently. Our old hearts will always want to determine what we need, leading us to chase after many things, but the Lord wants us above all to die to ourselves, carry our cross daily, and be totally dependent on Him. Do we truly trust him to provide the Bread that we need (Jn 6:22-71), and are we content to be branches on the Vine, which is Christ himself (Jn 15:1-16)? Do we walk in the Spirit (Rom 8:1-27) and is the fruit of the Spirit evident in our lives (Gal 5:13-26)? This isn't just about acting the right way, but it is also about every inclination of our heart (1 Cor 10:23-11:1). We are told "Be perfect, as your heavenly Father is perfect" (Mt 5:48). From what we learned in this level, is this perfection a matter of following the Law to a "T," or does it have more to do with our will's true surrender and dependence on a trustworthy God, even though he doesn't force us to?

Day 7. Level Seven – Matthew 7:21-23

The Lord will guide a believer and reveal his will using circumstances, friends, family, worship, prayer, the prompting of the Holy Spirit, and the Word of God—the Word that tells us, in Micah 6:8, that the Lord requires us "to do justice, and to love kindness, and to walk humbly with your God." Discerning these things and walking humbly with God sounds easy enough, but unless we can sacrifice our selfish wants and desires unto death, and truly allow our minds to be transformed/renewed (Rom 12:1-2), then His will becomes harder to determine. Someone who is used to operating at the first level (without "health and wealth" payoff) may feel that the Lord is letting them down. After all, haven't they been active in his causes? They may cry, "Lord, Lord, did we not prophesy in your name, and cast out demons in your name, and do many mighty works in your name?" But Jesus has said he "will declare to them, 'I never knew you; depart from me, you workers of lawlessness,'" because "Not everyone who says to me, 'Lord, Lord,' will enter the kingdom of heaven, but the one who does the will of my Father who is in heaven" (Mt 7:21-23).

We can do mighty works and get things wrong. Or maybe we find ourselves at higher levels (2 and 6), exhibiting the faith of Abraham and other Old Testament heroes, but then we read in 1 Corinthians 13:2 that "if I have all faith, so as to remove mountains, but have not love, I am nothing." Or perhaps, at levels 3 and 4, we follow Christ in giving up our lives, or, contrary to the example of the rich young ruler, we sell all we have and give to the poor. Isn't that enough? But then we read in 1 Corinthians 13:3 that "if I give away all I have, and if I deliver up my body to be burned, but have not love, I gain nothing." Christ's death would have meant nothing without the power of His perfect love for us. In the same way, all that we have ever done could mean nothing without love, and apart from abiding in Christ "you can do nothing" (Jn 15:5). To truly discern God's will, everything that we do should be for the glory of God (1 Cor 10:31), while abiding in Christ, and with love.

One of the most powerful forces on the earth and in heaven is love. In 1 Corinthians 13, we learn about love—the things that love is (and is not). It points out the splendor of patience, kindness, humility, endurance and sacrifice in our relationships. And that note of sacrifice is amplified in John 15:13: "Greater love has no one than this, that someone lay down his life for his friends." This is a one-and-done sort of service, one in which you retain none of your worldly possessions, career aspirations, or dreams for a comfortable and socially gratifying future on earth. It gives witness to a radical form of love. As Christians we consistently point to the great love of Jesus as the moment that He died for mankind. We are so busy "loving" ourselves, "loving" things, and even "loving" others that we don't realize the greatest way we can show love is to put to death all our selfish dreams, wants, and desires for the good of someone else, and love them while doing it.

The greatest love that we say God ever showed us was when he ceased to live and breathe on this earth. Not when he gave us what we wanted, not when he made us feel good, but when he ceased to breathe. God asks something similar of us. As with Naaman (2 Kgs 5:1-19), we refuse to submit and are so busy with good things, even great and holy things, that we just can't lay it all down and do what He asks. You want to show love to others? Be willing to put all those things that you want and you desire to death and don't utter a word of them to others. Lay down your life for your friends. Lay down your life for your spouse. Lay down your life for your enemies, even when they are cheating you, using you, deceiving you, and spitting in your face. Yes, of course, there is a time to stand against evil in the world, to be an instrument of justice and mercy for the abused, but you must not join in these efforts out of petulance or sheer hatred of the offenders. You must always consult the counsel of love, insistent that your act flows from a beneficent heart, and that, in the end, you wish the best for all concerned. Stop trying to prove yourself and stop defending yourself. Yes, Paul would occasionally respond to those who sought to shut down his ministry, but the point was not the preservation of his honor and safety. Rather, he was defending the cause of the gospel. Like Paul, we must be willing to take up our cross daily, even going to our own execution (Gal 2:19-21), and with a loving heart. That's the example of Christ.

Anyone can say that God is leading them to learn something on this level, but the only one who will really know that is true is the Lord himself, and we need to always be careful that we are not being led astray by our own wants and desires, or by the Prince of This World (Jn 14:30-31). Many evils of the world have been justified and committed in the name of God (genocide, slavery, cults, false messiahs, etc.) by those operating with the content in levels 1 to 4. Levels 5, 6 and 7 begin to reveal how we all have blind spots in our lives, seethe with discontentment, have uncontrollable wants and desires, and rebel against God by nature. Deep down we humans want to declare, "God is dead," and crucify Him with the Pharisees. Providentially, God has obliged us in a total act of surrender on Calvary. But then he used that same act to flip the wisdom of the world on its head, compel millions to surrender themselves to his will, and give him the glory he deserves. He overcame the world and changed everything through keeping his mouth shut in response to the false accusations at his trial and letting sinful men lead him to his death. And love, both for friends and enemies, was his overarching motivation.

We should pay attention to the power this type of sacrifice has to change the hearts of men, and throw everything at the feet of Jesus to show him we understand what he tried to teach us. Anything less is just trying to get the self-serving and self-preserving things we want and to do things in our own power to exercise independence from God. The goal of discipleship is not to be a "somebody" for Christ or even a "nobody" for Christ. It is rather to submit to him in humble obedience, partaking of his boundless love, content with whatever role, circumstances, and lifespan he may have in mind for us. That is how we become "somebodies" according to His Kingdom economy, whatever the world's estimation may be. As it is written in Romans 12:1-2, by presenting your body as a "living sacrifice" and allowing the "renewal of your mind" to take place, you can discern God's will. The ongoing surrender, dependence, and abiding in Christ that this requires makes it no easy task and not one that we can afford to take lightly. Indeed, many who think they know Christ will be told, "I never knew you." But those who truly understand these Seven Levels, and their own hearts, will not be surprised by this. Still, they probably won't even totally trust themselves, because, like Jesus, they "know what is in man" (Jn 2:24-25). But if this feels overwhelming, just remember, "Above all, keep loving one another earnestly, since love covers a multitude of sins," (1 Pt 4:8; Mt 22:37-40) and "whoever does not receive the kingdom of God like a child shall not enter it" (Lk 18:17).

CHAPTER 19

Seven Levels Guide

T he Bible is the most important book that has ever been written, because it was sent by God. But for someone who picks up the Bible for the first time, it can be difficult to know where to start. And even if you read it all the way through, it might be hard to see how it all fits together. You could study the Bible for a lifetime and not understand all of it, but there are certain overarching concepts that can help us frame our understanding of Scripture. Then we can more easily categorize the lessons we learn in an order that might help us bring them to mind on a daily basis. This is one of the purposes of these Seven Levels. It is also a practical tool to help us understand the direction our lives should head as we are made into disciples of Christ, and how we can bring glory to God and "pursue what makes for peace and for mutual upbuilding" (Rom 14:19). Being able to choose passages and stories from each of the levels to form a deeper understanding of every level will hopefully provide a fluid and flexible means of organizing our ongoing Bible study as we face heart challenges and spiritual growth in our daily lives.

Life as a follower of Christ is not meant to be lived alone but, rather, within a community. If we are discipling someone, we must also truly be a brother or sister in Christ to them, not satisfied to get together only when we want to study the Word of God. If that is our only contact with them, they can understandably come to think that we don't have their best interests at heart. We need to show our love and care for other areas of their life as well. As friends, we should understand the challenges others are facing and take time to discuss them as we support one another. This is when we show spiritual fruit in our own lives and see spiritual fruit in the lives of others. There might also be times that we work together on certain projects and get involved in each other's daily lives in other ways. It would be a tragedy if a new follower of Jesus left his former community of friends and immediately felt alone when he decided to become a follower of Jesus. Believers must play the role of family members in the community of faith in which they are involved.

1. **Our most important needs are not health, safety, and prosperity, but the need to be considered justified in our decisions in the eyes of man and God.**
   Belief in the temporal power of Christ in this world and his priority on forgiveness

Jesus had power to do anything he wanted while on earth, but he considered giving forgiveness of sins more important than any physical or temporal blessing (Lk 5:17-26, 7:36-50). This level can be used to identify those who believe Jesus did many miracles when He was on earth and is concerned about mankind's finding God's forgiveness. The forgiveness and miracles in these stories were only temporary and not yet eternal. Followers of other religions may believe these stories.

1. Mark 4:35-41, **Calming of a Storm.** Power over nature, but storms will come again.
2. Mark 5:1-20, **Freedom for a Demoniac.** Power over spirit world, but demons may possess or oppress again.
3. Mark 5:25-34, **Healing of a Bleeding Woman.** Power over sickness, but people get sick again.
4. Mark 5:35-43, **Rising of Jairus's Daughter.** Power over death, but people die again.
5. Luke 5:17-26, **Forgiven Paralyzed Man.** Power to forgive sins; secondarily, to heal.
6. Luke 7:36-50, **Forgiven Sinful Woman.** Forgiveness for sexual sin; greater need produces greater love.
7. Luke 18:9-14, **Forgiven Tax Collector.** Forgiveness for corruption, where the key is humility.

2. **By the measurements of religious law, we are all considered unworthy, and we are not justified in the decisions we have made in the eyes of either man or God. We must truly believe this.**
   Belief in the seriousness of sin, mankind's depravity, and the history of God's people

God's people, Israel, were the descendants of Jacob, and He made them his by bringing them out of Egypt through his power and the blood of lambs, and he gave them his Law (Ex 6, 12, 19-20). Because of the Fall, man is spiritually and morally broken, and so must offer up continual, temporary, blood sacrifices to acknowledge sin, with no final resolution in sight. This level reflects those who believe God created mankind, that he has a specific purpose for them and is accomplishing it in a specific way. These people believe that the Old Testament has authority and that God worked through the prophets and mediators to create a nation for Himself from the descendants of Abraham, Isaac, and Jacob. There are also prophecies about a Savior who will come to earth. Here are the basic lessons on the seriousness of sin, the role of blood sacrifice, and the way that sins can be forgiven.

1. Genesis 1-2, **Creation.** God created everything including man; we have a purpose and we are his.
   a. Genesis 3, **Choice and Fall.** Sin entered the world and explains the corruption of God's good creation.
2. Genesis 12, **Abraham's Call.** Promises to Abraham; faith; and a plan to bless the whole world through him.
   a. Genesis 22:1-19, **Abraham's Sacrifice.** Faithfulness when we don't understand; blood sacrifice still required.
3. Exodus 1, **Background to Moses.** God does not forget his people.
   a. Exodus 2-4, **Moses, Burning Bush, Lack of Trust.** God chooses his prophets and his plan goes his way according to his timing.
4. Exodus 6,12, **Passover and Freedom for Israel.** Importance of blood sacrifice; God creates his people and promises land.
   a. Exodus 19-20, **Israel at Mount Sinai.** Moses receives the Law of God in spite of Israel's being drawn to other gods.
5. 2 Samuel 7, **Promise to David.** God's plan and future kingdom; David's unworthiness and posture before God.
   a. 2 Samuel 11, **David and Bathsheba.** Prophets sin, but God still uses them; sin crouching.
   b. 2 Samuel 12, **Nathan's Story.** The importance of repentance (see also Ps 51).
6. 2 Chronicles 36:15-21, **Babylonian Captivity.** God punishes his people, controls nations.
   a. Daniel 6; 7:13-14, **Daniel and the Lion's Den.** God is still with his people in hard times.
7. Nehemiah 1; 6:15-16; 8-9, **Nehemiah Rebuilds Jerusalem Wall.** God restores his people, though they're still slaves.

a. Isaiah 52-53, **Promise.** Prophecies of the Promised One, who will be a Suffering Servant.

3. **Only when we truly believe and admit that we are wrong/unjustified in the decisions we have made, and have no defense, and repent of our sinful thinking and acting, will God declare us justified. We are then born again as justified humans and have the potential to develop into genuine disciples of Christ.**
   Belief that Christ's death created the true people of God, and conviction regarding the importance of knowing and surrendering to Christ's voice

Through the life, death, and blood of the Lamb of God, Jesus, the first sinless descendant of Jacob, and the fulfiller of the Old Testament promises, those who surrender their lives to him and know his voice will receive eternal forgiveness of their sins. Through his resurrection and victory over death, we can be born again to obey the heart of the Law of God with a pure heart (1 Cor 15:1-8; Jn 10). This level presupposes the content of levels 1 and 2, which explain why Jesus had to come and how his death could save mankind. The hearer will then need to decide what kind of spiritual "soil" they are after hearing these stories and learning that some will be saved (and some burned) based on whether they have surrendered to the Shepherd and know his voice. This is about humility, surrender, and trust. The result primarily concerns the heart and allegiance, not mere intellectual assent to propositions.

1. Matthew 1:18-25, Luke 2, **Birth of Jesus.** Virgin birth and fulfiller of prophecies.
2. Luke 18:15-17, 31-42, **Sight.** Anticipates crucifixion of Jesus; prescribes faith like child.

a. Luke 19:28-44, 47-8, **Triumphal Entry of Jesus.** Jesus is received with joy and is seen as the fulfiller of prophecies. Soon after, he is rejected.

3. Luke 23, Matthew 26, 27, **Arrest & Trial of Jesus.** Jealousy of religious leaders, Jesus' silence in the face of false accusations.

4. Luke 23:32-56, **Crucifixion of Jesus.** Jesus lays down his life for the world. He is in control and shows us what we must do while he is simultaneously doing everything.

5. Luke 24, Matthew 28, Acts 1, **Resurrection of Jesus.** Jesus overcomes death (1 Cor 15:1-19) to show that we are in capable hands and that he rules.

6. Mark 4:1-20, **The Four Soils.** There are different ways that people receive and respond to the good news about Jesus.
   a. Matthew 13:24-30, 36-43, **The Wheat and the Tares.** Those committed to self are mixed in with those committed to surrender; God knows which are which.

7. Luke 14:25-33, **Cost of Discipleship.** Becoming a disciple demands sacrifice, trust, and hardship. Not a light decision.
   a. John 10, **The Good Shepherd.** Not just belief in facts. Trust him, know his voice. Jesus is One with God.

4. **After we have been justified through Christ, we will often still continue trying to justify ourselves in the eyes of man and God, but as we develop into disciples of Christ, our hearts and minds will transform.**
The belief that a follower of Christ should be humble, forgiving, loving, and obedient to him

This begins the training of what it means to be a distinctive follower of Jesus. We show that we are the people of God if we forgive others as we were forgiven and if we love Christ through obeying His commands, loving God, and others. It is important for believers to be obedient to Christ to show that they are truly his followers, but this obedience is not simply about honoring the behavioral directives the Lord gives us. As you'll see, the first three parables listed below deal with matters of the *heart*, and then the last four are theological lessons combined with practical actions, which are also a part of discipleship. Spiritual growth and development in becoming like Christ require primary attention to the higher levels, but, unfortunately, many will return to a striving to obey the written law in order to obtain health, safety, prosperity, or other blessings from God. Of course, we should trust God for these things, and it is not wrong to desire them, but they should not be our focus. We should learn to trust and love God and others when he takes those good things away, just as Christ showed us.

1. Matthew 18:23-35, **The Unforgiving Servant.** Our incomparable willingness to forgive, following God's model.
2. Matthew 19:16-30, **The Rich Man.** The Law does not justify, but fully trusting in God does. Poverty can be instructive.
3. Matthew 25:14-30, **The Talents.** We have different gifts and are responsible to take risks in stewardship and obedience.
4. John 3:1-21, **Jesus and Nicodemus.** We are born of the Spirit and water.
   a. Matthew 3:11-17, **Jesus' Baptism.** Obedience in baptism (Rom 6:1-11).
5. Mark 7:1-23, Acts 17:11, **Word and Traditions.** (Rv 22:18-19). Word (2 Tm 3:15-17; Heb 4:12) has precedence over tradition.
   a. Matthew 6:5-18, **Jesus in Prayer before Key Events.** Prayer (Mk 1:35-45; Lk 6:12-19) with a persistent heart (Lk 18:1-8); prayer and fasting that pleases God (Mt 6:5-18).
6. 1 Corinthians 12:12-31, **The Body of Christ.** (Acts 2:37-47). Function of church as a Christian community, with complementary roles (Rom 12:3-21).

    a. Luke 22:14-23, **Last Supper, Bread.** (Jn 6:52-71). Lord's Supper (1 Cor 11:23-34) as ongoing church practice.

7. John 13:1-20, **Foot Washing, Being Great.** (Mt 20:20-28). Humble Service (Lk 22:24-27).

    a. John 14:15-27, **The Holy Spirit and Obedience.** Producing and revealing love for Christ.

    b. 1 Corinthians 13:1-13, **The Greatest of These is Love.** Unique role and quality of love in Christianity.

5. **The church is the context in which we learn that people of all races and backgrounds can be justified in Christ, and that they do not gain salvation from righteous behavior, group identity, or the approval of others.**

The belief in the primacy and equality of God's grace for all races, with Christ ruling above all

Salvation was originally for the Jews, but through Christ it became available to people of all nations, tribes, and languages on earth—the new Family of God. The head of this Family, Jesus, was not just a sinless Jew, but preeminently the Last Adam, True High Priest, the King of Kings, and the very Word of God (Mk 3:31-35; Rom 5:12-21; Heb 3; Rv 20:1-10; Jn 1:1-29). This level identifies people who understand the plan of God for the world, who are members of a new family locally, and are part of the universal church throughout the world and its ages. They must be willing to sacrifice and receive believers from different people groups and nations as brothers and sisters in Christ. The extent to which we sacrifice for others, spend time with them, and humble ourselves will often show what we truly think about them. This level deals with understanding the mission of God, our role in discipleship, and the glory and power of Jesus. Jesus will return as King of Kings in this world—the High Priest and God Incarnate.

1. Romans 10:9-21, **God found us while we were sinners.** Saves all who call on him, drawing them to himself first.
   a. Matthew 28:18-20, **The Great Commission.** The Discipleship Plan of Jesus.
   b. Acts 1-2, **Ends of the Earth, Pentecost.** Holy Spirit; Many Languages; Jesus with us.
2. Acts 9-10, **Paul meets Jesus; Peter's Vision.** God declares the unclean as clean. Gospel and Spirit for Non-Jews.
3. Acts 16-17, 1 Thessalonians 2-3, **Paul and Silas Accepted, Resisted.** Geographical advance of the Church; Greece.
   a. Acts 19-20, Colossians 2-3, **Paul in Ephesus; Church Growth.** Heart in ministry and facing persecution; Turkey.
4. Mark 3:31-35, **New Family.** (Mk 1:16-20). Surrogate Family (1 Cor 6:1-8) should be the role of the church.
   a. Romans 8:28-10:4, **The Elect of God, Chosen.** (1 Thes 1). Holy Priesthood (1 Pt 1:1-2:12); new identity as chosen believer.
5. Revelation 1-3, 20:11-15, **Churches Evaluated and Judgment.** Church as the Bride of Christ (Eph 5:22-33; Rv 19:7-9); Mystery.
   a. Hebrews 3, **High Priest.** (Heb 7:23-28; 9:11-28). Jesus is Forever Priest and Mediator.
6. John 1:1-29, Hebrews 1, **The Word is God; Angels Worship Him.** The Lamb of God and Creator.
   a. Colossians 1:15-23, **Supremacy of Christ.** (1 Cor 15:20-58). One Man; Second Adam (Rom 5:12-21).
7. Revelation 20, 22:6-21, **Christ's Reign; War; Judgment.** Second Coming (1 Thes 4:13-5:11) of Jesus, establishing his rule.
   a. Revelation 7:9-17; 21-22:6, **New Heavens, New Earth.** Hope in the afterlife; No more suffering.

6. **For the sake of vital truth rather than mere personal vindication, Christ and His Apostles could be seen to set the record straight when false accusations were hurled at them, but we must understand that our saving justification in Christ should empower us to have peace when others seek to justify themselves, even when it is at our expense. Because we are free with respect to all, we make ourselves servants to all. This is the example of Christ.**
The belief in the power of self-sacrifice, even for enemies, and finding sufficiency in God

A key to becoming like Christ is to realize that our personal wants and desires are the main thing keeping us from surrendering to the will of God. If we are not able in true humility to put our wants to death and be at peace when others (even the most evil persons) get the better of us, we can never reach perfection in the eyes of God (Rom 7:7-25; Gal 2:19-21; Mt 5:1-48). These deeper and more difficult teachings will be a challenge to live up to throughout the life of each believer. An understanding of our wants and desires, of what we can control, of our need for self-sacrifice, and the call to be content in all situations is very important in this category.

1. Romans 5:6-11, **We are His Enemies and have Rejected Him.** (Jn 5:18-47). Theologians of the Cross (Gal 2:19 21) believe all must die to self before God; he makes us new, not just better.

2. Romans 4, **Abraham righteous by Faith.** Righteousness before the Law cannot result from following the Law. We break it, and Law demands we die.

   a. Luke 16:19-31, **Rich Man and Lazarus, Faith Heroes.** Believe the unseen; exercise faith (Heb 11).

3. Romans 7:7-25, **Law and Sin.** Struggles to obey will last our whole life. Concentration on the Law does not advance our pursuit of righteousness but hinders us.

4. Romans 8:1-27, **Walk in the Spirit.** (Gal 5:13-26). Our lives should evidence the fruit of the Spirit, not deeds of the flesh; the two are in conflict within us.

5. John 15:1-16, **Vine and Branches.** We must abide in Christ, not live independently. Nothing we do should be apart from him.

6. John 6:22-51, **Bread of Life; Jesus is True Food.** Contentment (Phil 4:11-13; 1 Cor 7) should mark our lives regardless of circumstances, because in hardship we can show trust in him and not idols.

7. Matthew 5:1-48, **Perfect Man.** Our pursuit of perfection, which he commands, is not centered on the letter of the Law. It is marked by grace, mercy, humility and a clear vision of ourselves (1 Cor 10:23-11:1).

7. **When we truly understand in our hearts that we have been justified at our core by God through Christ, even though we have all been proven wrong and are not justified according to the Law, we are finally able to live an unhindered, full life, capable of pure trust and sacrifice with love and thankfulness. Justification sets us free to worship God in a way superior to Adam's.**
Belief in the importance of love, trust, and dependence to discern God's will

If we truly believe all the Word of God, trust in his plan, surrender to and obey Christ, die to ourselves, and consider others better than ourselves, but still not do these things with true love for them and God in our hearts, then it amounts to nothing in the eyes of God (1 Cor 13:1-3; Mt 22:37-40). This level shows that no matter how great our sacrifices and accomplishments in the name of God, if they are not done in love, they count for nothing. This seemingly impossible requirement is undergirded by God's assurance that full dependence on him as his child should be our mindset.

1. Matthew 7:21-23, **Mighty Acts in God's Name.** Despite impressive accomplishments, some will hear Jesus say, "I never knew you," for their achievements give no evidence of vital relationship with the Shepherd.

2. 1 Corinthians 13:1-3, **Mighty Acts without Love.** They are nothing. Self-sacrificial and faithful love is the engine that should power everything we do.

3. John 2:23-25, **Jesus Knows Man.** Man's depravity fuels his tendency to listen to the Prince of the World (Jn 14:30-31). Do not fool yourself about what Jesus knows about you.

4. John 8:28-29, **Pleasing the Father.** Jesus was and is with the Father, both divine and submissive.

5. Romans 12:1-2, **Discerning the Will of God.** We must have a transformed and renewed mind to determine God's will. We must beware of defining righteousness in the world's terms.

6. John 15:12-14, **Greatest Love.** The greatest act of love is not to do things for others, but to die for them for the sake of the gospel, as Christ did (Gal 2:19-21).

   a. 2 Kings 5:1-19, **Naaman.** We must humble ourselves to submit to the simplicity of God's commands, which honor him, not ourselves.

7. Matthew 22:37-40, **Greatest Commandment.** The simplicity and difficulty of the greatest commandments require deep relationships with God and others. Love covers sins (1 Pt 4:8).

   a. Luke 18:17, **Receive the Kingdom as if a Child.** Despite the apparent difficulty in becoming who God wants us to be, the key is radically simple. Total dependence and trust in God as if by a child.

About the Author

The author has called Buton home for over 16 years, along with his wife Tiffany, and children Alethia, Asher, and Adriel. He has managed a tourism company that provides tours throughout Buton and the surrounding islands since 2010, and recently completed his master's degree in Sustainable Tourism. He also has master's degrees in cross-cultural studies and theology and has led several community development projects on these islands. He has published two books about Buton, *The Mysteries of the Islands of Buton* and *South Buton and the Womb of Eastern Indonesian Islam*. He has also published three case studies about tourism on Buton in the academic *Journal of Hospitality and Tourism Cases* which is published by the International Council on Hotel, Restaurant, and Institutional Education (ICHRIE). He currently resides in Auburn, AL with his family.

Endnotes

1   M. N. Ardani, "Kepemilikan Hak Atas Tanah Bagi Orang Asing di Indonesia (Land Ownership for Foreigners in Indonesia)," *Journal Law Reform* 13, no. 2 (2017): 204-216.

2   O. Pye, I. Radjawali, and Julia, "Land grabs and the river: eco-social transformations along the Kapuas, Indonesia." *Canadian Journal of Development Studies* 38, no. 3 (2017): 378-394.

3   E. Agustina, "The Social Function of Land Rights in Indonesia: The Basic Agrarian Law and Customary Rights by the State." *Journal of Legal, Ethical and Regulatory Issues (Special Issue*, 2018*)* 21: 1-8.

4   Leon Morris, *The Gospel According to St. Luke* (Grand Rapids, MI: William B. Eerdmans Publishing Co., 1974), 248-249.

5   Ibid., 248.

6   John Sailhamer, *NIV Compact Bible Commentary* (Grand Rapids, MI: Zondervan Publishing House, 1994), 479.

7   Caleb T. Coppenger, *South Buton and the Womb of Eastern Indonesian Islam* (San Diego, CA: Aventine Press, 2020), Chapter 7.

Chapter 1

8   Awaluddin, "State's Authority Rights Over Land in Indonesia," *Tadulako Law Review* 2, no. 2 (December 2017): 107-123.

9   Y. Liu and F. Yamauchi, "Population density, migration, and the returns to human

capital and land: Insights from Indonesia," *Food Policy* 48 (2014): 182-193.

10   *The Star*, "Indonesia land quandary," Last modified September 28, 2018. Johannesburg (p. 27).

11   Giles Milton, *Nathaniel's Nutmeg* (New York: Farrar, Straus, and Giroux, 1999).

12   Coppenger, *The Mysteries of the Islands of Buton* (San Diego, CA: Aventine Press, 2011).

13   J. Adam, "Downward social mobility, prestige and the informal economy in post-conflict Ambon," *South East Asia Research* 16, no. 3 (November 2008): 461-479.

14   Palmer, Blair D. "Big Men and Old Men: Migrant-Led Status Change in Buton, Indonesia." PhD Diss., Australian National University, December 2009.

15   M. A. K. Sahide and L. Giessen, "The fragmented land use administration in Indonesia – Analysing bureaucratic responsibilities influencing tropical rainforest transformation systems." *Land Use Policy* 43 (2015): 96-110.

16   P. I. Rietberg and O. Hospes, "Unpacking land acquisition at the oil palm frontier: Obscuring customary rights and local authority in West Kalimantan, Indonesia," *Asia Pacific Viewpoint* 59, no. 3 (2018): 338-348.

17   Brockhaus, M., K. Obidzinski, A. Dermawan, Y. Laumonier, and C. Luttrell. "An overview of forest and land allocation policies in Indonesia: Is the current framework sufficient to meet the needs of REDD+?" *Forest Policy and Economics* 18 (2012): 30-37; Harahap, F., S. Silveira, and D. Khatiwada. "Land allocation to meet sectoral goals in Indonesia – An analysis of policy coherence." *Land Use Policy* 61 (2017): 451-465.

18   M. Indrawan, J. Caldecott, and Ermayanti, "Mitigating Tensions over Land Conversion in Papua, Indonesia," *Asia & the Pacific Policy Studies* 4, no. 1 (January 2017), 150.

19   Berenschot, W. Book Review on *Land and Development in Indonesia: Searching for the People's Sovereignty* by John McCarthy & Kathryn Robinson (Eds). *Bijdragen Tot de Taal-, Land- en Volkenkunde* 174, no. 2-3 (2018): 328-332.

20   Hendrartyo, M. "Walhi Reveals 82 Percent of Land Controlled by Corporations." *Tempo* (2018) Retrieved from https://en.tempo.co/read/news/2018/03/23/055916921/Walhi-Reveals-82-Percent-of-Land -Controlled-by-Corporations.

21   Agustina.

22 F. Amelia, J. Iskandar, R. Partasmita, and N. Malone. "Recognizing indigenous knowledge of the Karangwangi Rural Landscape in South Cianjur, Indonesia for sustainable land management." *Biodiversitas* 19, no. 5 (September 2018): 1722-1729.

23 S. Steinebach and Y. Kunz, "Separating Sisters from Brothers: Ethnic Relations and Identity Politics in the Context of Indigenous Land Titling in Indonesia." *ASEAS* 10, no. 1 (2017): 47-63.

24 T. M. Li, *Land's End: Capitalist Relations on an Indigenous Frontier* (Durham, NC: Duke University Press, 2014).

25 Tamsil, Susilowati, I. F., and M. Wardhana. "Perspective of public law in rearrangement of profit-sharing system agricultural land in Indonesia." *Journal of Physics: Conference Series* 953 (2018): 1-5.

26 J. A. Hartanto, "Legal Aspects of Land Purchase/Sale Disputes in Indonesia," *Environmental Policy and Law* 48, no. 1 (2018): 79-82.

27 W. van der Muur, "Forest conflicts and the informal nature of realizing indigenous land rights in Indonesia." *Citizenship Studies* 22, no. 2 (2018): 160-174.

28 P. C. Timmer, "The road to pro-poor growth: the Indonesian experience in regional perspective," *Bulletin of Indonesian Economic Studies* 40, no. 2 (2004): 177-207.

29 Krishna, V. V., C. Kubitza, U. Pascual, and M. Qaim. "Land markets, Property rights, and Deforestation: Insights from Indonesia." *World Development* 99 (2017): 335-349.

30 *The Star.*

31 Ardani.

32 *Indonesia-Investments.* "How to Establish a Foreign Company (PT PMA) in Indonesia?" (2023). Retrieved from https://www.indonesia-investments.com/business/foreigninvestment/establish-foreign-company-pt-pma/item5739?

33 Achsan, F. "Kepemilikan Hak Atas Tanah Oleh Warga Negara Asing Melalui Perjanjian Nominee." *Kumparan* (April 17, 2018). Retrieved from https://kumparan.com/ferriz-achsan/kepemilikan-hak-atas-tanah-oleh-warga-negara-asing-melalui-perjanjian-nominee.

34 T. R. Slaper and T. J. Hall, "The triple bottom line: What is it and how does it work?" *Indiana Business Review* 86, no. 1 (2011): 4-8.

35 WTO, *Manila Declaration on World Tourism* (Madrid: World Tourism Organization, 1998), 21.

36 J. Duclos, "What is "Pro-Poor"?" *Social Choice Welfare* 32 (2009): 37-58. Springer-Verlag.

37 Kakwani, K., S. Khandker, and H. H. Son. (2004). "Pro-poor growth: Concepts and measurement with country case studies." *International Poverty Center Working Paper No. 1*. Brasilia: United Nations Development Programme International Poverty Centre, 2004.

38 D. Harrison, "Pro-poor Tourism: a critique," *Third World Quarterly* 29, no. 5 (2008): 851-868.

39 S. Klasen & Reimers, M. (2017). "Looking at Pro-Poor Growth from an Agricultural Perspective." *World Development 90*, 147-168.

40 E. T. Byrd, "Stakeholders in sustainable tourism development and their roles: applying stakeholder theory to sustainable tourism development. *Tourism Review* 62, no. 2 (2007): 6-13.

41 P. Wulandari and S. Kassim. "Issues and challenges in financing the poor: case of Baitul Maal Wa Tamwil in Indonesia." *International Journal of Bank Marketing* 34, no. 2 (2016): 216-234.

42 L. Twining-Ward and R. Butler, "Implementing STD on a Small Island: Development and Use of Sustainable Tourism Development Indicators in Samoa," *Journal of Sustainable Tourism* 10, no. 5 (2002): 363-387.

43 D. W. Knight, "An institutional analysis of local strategies for enhancing pro-poor tourism outcomes in Cuzco, Peru," *Journal of Sustainable Tourism* 26, no. 4 (2018): 631-648.

44 R. Kanbur and G. Rauniyar, "Conceptualizing inclusive development: with applications to rural infrastructure and development assistance," *Journal of the Asia Pacific Economy* 15, no. 4 (2010): 437-454.

45 A. W. Handaru, "Pro-Poor Tourism: Findings from Bangka Island, Indonesia," *Academy of Strategic Management Journal* 17, no. 2 (2018): 1-10.

Chapter 4

46 Steve Corbett and Brian Fikkert, *When Helping Hurts* (Chicago: Moody Publishers, 2009), 28.

47 Kahlil Gibran, *The Prophet* (NY: Alfred Knopf, 1923), 55.

48 Sean Peek, "What is Social Entrepreneurship?" US Chamber of Commerce (July 30, 2020). Accessed May 21, 2023. https://www.uschamber.com/co/startup/

what-is-social-entrepreneurship.

49   *The Economist*, "Triple bottom line," (November 17, 2009).

50   Matt Rhodes, *No Shortcut to Success: A Manifesto for Modern Missions* (Wheaton, IL: Crossway, 2022), Chapter 4.

51   Ibid., Chapter 8.

Chapter 7

52   Akeptus, "Leaving the World a Better Place than How We Found It" Akeptus (April 26, 2019). Accessed Jan 11, 2024. https://medium.com/builddie/leaving-the-world-a-better-place-than-how-we-found-it-7b375b8475e9

53   Alex and Brett Harris, *Do Hard Things: A Teenage Rebellion Against Low Expectations* (Colorado Springs, CO: WaterBrook & Multnomah, 2008).

54   Mel Tari, *Like a Mighty Wind* (Green Forest, AR: New Leaf Press, 1995).

Chapter 9

55   Barry Asmus and Wayne Grudem, *The Poverty of Nations: A Sustainable Solution* (Wheaton, IL: Crossway, 2013).

56   Marvin Olasky, *The Tragedy of American Compassion* (Washington, D.C.: Regnery Publishing, 1994).

Chapter 10

57   Gibran, 22.

Chapter 11

58   John Stott, *The Cross of Christ* (Downers Grove, IL: Intervarsity Press, 1986), 179.

59   Ibid., 180.

60   Ibid., 191.

61   Paul Coelho, *The Alchemist* (London: Thorsons, 1988).

62   John Piper, *Providence* (Wheaton, IL: Crossway, 2021), 584.

Chapter 13

63   Jonathan Haidt, *The Righteous Mind: Why Good People are Divided by Politics and Religion* (NT: Vintage Books, 2013), Chapter 4.

Chapter 15

64 Gerhard O. Forde, *On Being a Theologian of the Cross: Reflections on Luther's Heidelberg Disputation, 1518* (Grand Rapids, MI: William B. Eerdmans Publishing Co, 1997).

65 Bill Hull, *The Disciple-Making Pastor: Leading Others on the Journey of Faith* (Grand Rapids, MI: Baker Books, 1988).

Chapter 18

66 Joseph H. Hellerman, *When the Church Was a Family: Recapturing Jesus' Vision for Authentic Christian Community* (Nashville, TN: B&H Publishing Group, 2009).

A free ebook edition is available with the purchase of this book.

To claim your free ebook edition:

1. Visit MorganJamesBOGO.com
2. Sign your name CLEARLY in the space
3. Complete the form and submit a photo of the entire copyright page
4. You or your friend can download the ebook to your preferred device

Morgan James BOGO™

A **FREE** ebook edition is available for you or a friend with the purchase of this print book.

CLEARLY SIGN YOUR NAME ABOVE

Instructions to claim your free ebook edition:
1. Visit MorganJamesBOGO.com
2. Sign your name CLEARLY in the space above
3. Complete the form and submit a photo of this entire page
4. You or your friend can download the ebook to your preferred device

Print & Digital Together Forever.

Snap a photo

Free ebook

Read anywhere

Printed in the USA
CPSIA information can be obtained
at www.ICGtesting.com
JSHW022006270824
68876JS00002B/9

9 781636 984001